THINK LIKE A CRIMINAL AND
ACT LIKE A LAWYER

CRIMINAL MINDSET

VAIBHAV YADAV

FOREWORD BY DR. VIKAS SINGH
PRESIDENT, SUPREME COURT BAR ASSOCIATION (SCBA)
AND FORMER ADDL SOLICITOR GENERAL OF INDIA

INDIA • SINGAPORE • MALAYSIA

ISBN
Paperback 979-8-89699-515-9
Hardcase 979-8-89961-855-0

Contents

Foreword

The dividing line between cunning and true brilliance is drawn by how firmly one respects the rules—and how shrewdly one wields them.

From my vantage point as a Senior Advocate at the Supreme Court of India, I've witnessed every shade of human ambition—from those who bend laws beyond moral recognition to those too hesitant to seize opportunities. ***Criminal Mindset: Think Like a Criminal and Act Like a Lawyer***, by **Vaibhav Yadav**, offers a fascinating and refreshing antidote to these extremes, proposing a path where daring strategy flourishes without forsaking ethical guardrails.

Vaibhav starts with the premise that criminals often possess a heightened sense of observation and impeccable timing, tapping into vulnerabilities that go unnoticed by most. Instead of glorifying lawlessness, he reframes these instincts through a legal lens—upholding accountability and discipline so that you may think boldly while remaining firmly on the right side of the law.

Whether in business, relationship, or life's countless unspoken contests, those who drift passively often become the prey. They walk into ambushes they never see coming.

In a world rife with quick shortcuts and fleeting gains, this approach stands out for its insistence on alignment with deeper values.

What truly distinguishes Criminal Mindset is Vaibhav's recognition of the moral dimension behind each calculated move. He demonstrates that a brilliant tactic, divorced from integrity, soon collapses under the weight of betrayal or legal sanction. In contrast, strategy grounded in accountability and heightened awareness achieves staying power, protecting both your ambitions and the principles you hold dear.

Whether you're an entrepreneur, a lawyer, or simply someone forging your path through complex negotiations, this book challenges you to sharpen your focus, master persuasion, and stay vigilant about the delicate boundary that distinguishes shrewdness from exploitation.

Through engaging narratives and practical lessons, Vaibhav champions the belief that power must serve genuine purpose, not merely personal gain.

Vaibhav's work dares to unify bold vision with lawful order. May Criminal Mindset spark in you the insight to see opportunity where others see only barriers— and the wisdom to pursue those opportunities with unwavering integrity.

Dr. VIKAS SINGH
Senior Advocate, Supreme Court of India
President
Supreme Court Bar Association
Former **Additional Solicitor General of India**

Preface

"A stalwart stands unbowed by storms, not because they are unyielding, but because they embrace each gust as a new call to strength."

Dedicated to the memory of my late grandfather (Bauji), Chaudhary Kanwar Singh Ji—a steadfast beacon who taught me that true courage is not the absence of fear, but the refusal to be paralyzed by it. He was a stalwart champion of ethical resolve, instilling in me the belief that goals are not simply pursued, but wrestled from adversity. May this book honor his legacy by echoing his relentless spirit and unwavering commitment to doing what is right, no matter the odds.

I am eternally indebted to my Chacha Ji, Ajay Veer Yadav, whose unshakeable resolve and unwavering encouragement illuminate every path I choose to tread. His belief in me endures as the quiet force propelling my ambition forward, reminding me that when the world feels unwelcoming or insurmountable, there is always hope to be found in the arms of unwavering support. Without his resolve, I would be lost in the noise of daily life. Without his perseverance, this book, and all that I aim to accomplish in life, would remain just a daydream.

I still recall my *grandfather* (Bauji)—sturdy in frame, gentle in spirit. In a world where formal learning was often a distant dream, he fought relentlessly for it, scraping together every resource until he carved out a path of knowledge for himself. To me, he was a living testament that no adversity is too great for a person whose resolve refuses to bow, whose mind rejects the notion of defeat. It was he who first kindled my ambition, urging me to pursue education with the same unflinching determination he wore like a second skin. He remained a steady anchor—proof that diligence, practicality and a solid moral footing can conquer the most daunting circumstances.

My *Chacha* Ji, Ajay Veer Yadav, embodies a quieter, yet equally profound, source of courage and support. Throughout my life, he has stood by with a silent nod of encouragement for dreams that must have, at times, seemed wildly impossible. Where others might question my leaps of ambition, he simply offered patience, embracing each plan—no matter how offbeat—so that I'd feel the thrill of exploration rather than the chill of doubt. His presence is a fortification: an iron-strong reasurance that I need never weather storms alone. It is not just my life that he's touched so deeply; many in his orbit have felt the warmth of his dedication. He appears tireless, continuously placing the needs of others above his own, staunchly refusing to bend before even the greatest adversities. The quiet impact of his humility resonates in all who know him, reminding me that genuine influence springs from serving others more than oneself.

If, through this book and my entire life, I manage to glean even a fraction of their greatness, it will be a personal triumph. While I dream of standing in the shadows of these extraordinary men, I know their feats of diligence, generosity and resolve form a pinnacle I may never fully reach. Their lessons—one exemplifying a fierce commitment to self-improvement and moral strength, the other embodying silent, selfless support—thread through every sentence I write here, weaving a tapestry of ambition tempered by responsibility.

Criminal Mindset: Think Like a Criminal and Act Like a Lawyer germinated from a single, paradoxical question: *Is it possible to channel the daring audacity often found in those who flout rules, while keeping one's moral anchor intact?* I recognized that a con artist's gift for spotting hidden angles can be inverted for constructive ends if paired with the disciplining framework of legal thought. Much as my grandfather fought to acquire knowledge so that adversity would never again corner him, and much as my Chacha Ji's silent fortitude shelters my own wild pursuits, this book proposes that cunning need not equate to lawlessness—rather, it can flourish under the right balance of discipline and decency.

When the seed of *Criminal Mindset* first began to sprout in my mind, I found myself grappling with a paradox that continues to fascinate me: *What if, in order to triumph in life's complex arenas, one must fuse the bold instincts of a predator with the structural safeguards of law?* It occurred to me that we often admire those who achieve astounding feats of power and prosperity, yet in the same breath condemn the morally ambiguous tactics that might have gotten them there. We stand entranced by the cunning of a legendary con artist, but recoil from their disregard for justice. Conversely, we revere the professionalism of the world's finest attorneys, but fail to appreciate how their rigorous frameworks can sometimes stifle bold innovation.

In this book, I set out to reconcile those extremes—bringing together *the daring insight of criminality* (one that sees opportunity even in locked doors) with *the protective discipline of the law* (the unwavering structure that defends us from harm, internal or external). By navigating these convergent paths, we discover a vantage that is startlingly powerful yet grounded in a conscientious sense of ethics. Through countless hours of research and reflection, through anecdotes and allegories drawn from history's greatest masterminds—both infamous and heroic—I have endeavored to present a framework that unlocks new ways of seeing the world.

Yet no such journey unfolds in a vacuum. My inspiration and perseverance trace back to the figures who first showed me that true strength radiates from the inside out. My grandfather, whose very presence spoke of resilience and moral fortitude, imparted a lesson that greatness emerges not simply from triumphs but also from the daily skirmishes we fight within ourselves. And my Chacha Ji—through his tireless affirmation—proved that no dream is too large, no aspiration too grand, if you have even one person who believes wholeheartedly in your possibilities.

For readers who come across these pages, I hope you discover more than a compilation of cunning techniques and legal insights. I hope you find an invitation to reframe your perspective on boundaries—both the ones we respect and the ones we dare to push. *Criminal Mindset* beckons you to question, to stretch, to reevaluate how you perceive obstacles and harness them for creative advantage. But most importantly, it nudges you to remember that power, devoid of conscience, is ultimately a self-collapsing illusion.

The first step to real power, then, is not only understanding that rules can be bent—it is knowing when *not* to bend them. May you read these words with a spark of daring, an appetite for innovation, and a loyalty to those values that guard our humanity. If my grandfather's ethics and my Chacha Ji's resolve have passed in part to me, I hope this book will pass a measure of the same forward to you—an enduring sense of courage entwined with heart.

And so, with gratitude, humility, and a deep reverence for the relentless pursuit of goals, I invite you to slip into these pages and contemplate the intersection where a criminal's brilliance and a lawyer's discipline meet. May you emerge emboldened, more aware, and ready to orchestrate your life's challenges with unprecedented vision.

May this work do justice to their memory and presence—and, in doing so, guide you to think more boldly, act more wisely, and embrace your own pursuits with the fierce but compassionate spirit they so effortlessly display.

– Vaibhav

Introduction

The Duality of Power

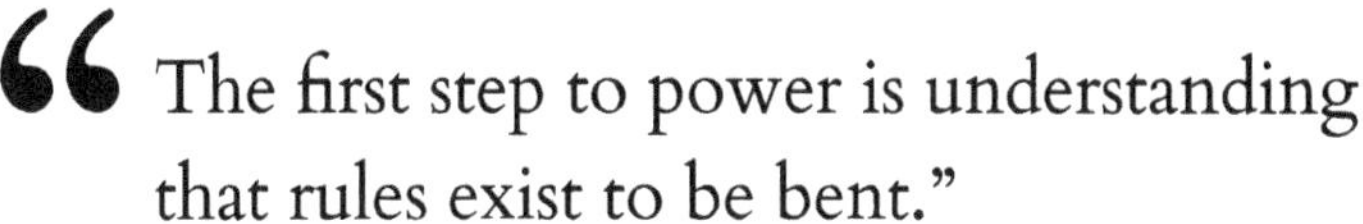

> "The first step to power is understanding that rules exist to be bent."

The figure stood poised at the edge of a dimly lit parking lot, black hood pulled low to conceal their face, while the neon hum of a flickering streetlamp cast a trembling circle of light on the crumbling asphalt. It was nearly midnight, and from the vantage point of any casual passerby, nothing about the scene seemed noteworthy. Just another hooded stranger hunched in the shadows, perhaps waiting for a ride that was running late or catching a breath of night air in solitude. But appearances are often the most convenient illusions. If one looked closer—truly looked—they might notice the rigid stillness of the shoulders, the measured pace of the breaths, and the methodical way the eyes scanned every angle of the parking lot. This was a person on a mission, and in the next few moments, the reality of that mission would collide with the boundaries we call "laws."

Behind the hood was a set of keen, restless eyes. Those eyes locked onto the distant silhouette of a once-stately courthouse, a place that in daylight carried the promise of justice but, in the hush of late night, stood like a silent fortress of secrets. The hooded figure's pulse quickened. A small device glinted in one gloved hand—a device for picking locks, an old skill refined through countless repetitions. The stakes were high, but the payoff was immense. Somewhere within those marble hallways and secured filing rooms lay a sealed folder containing the crucial evidence needed for a trial that was set to begin at sunrise. If this evidence vanished, the entire proceeding would tilt in favor of one side. If the figure succeeded, a man who might otherwise be convicted could walk free—or a guilty party could remain undetected. No one would know how it happened. No one would be able to pin the blame.

Moments later, as the figure stepped into the courthouse's dark corridor, there was no clumsy clatter, no hastily slammed door, no blaring alarm. Just soft footsteps and the near-silent click of a lock relenting under expert hands. By the time the night watchman made his predictable rounds, the figure was already gone. The only trace left behind, if one even dared to call it a trace, was a single empty folder where crucial documents had once been. Across town, in a tastefully furnished office, a young defense lawyer would soon discover that those exact documents—documents that could determine a client's fate—had miraculously appeared on his desk.

That story, whether fact or the stuff of urban legend, crackles with the essential theme of this book: the astonishing power that arises when we merge *criminal cunning* with *legal discipline*. What you have just witnessed is an illustration of **The Duality of Power**—the raw, risk-taking audacity of someone who dares to flout the rules, paired with the strategic intelligence of a lawyer poised to use newly acquired evidence within the formalities of law. One side orchestrates the stealth; the other wields the argument. One navigates the gray areas of the night; the other steps boldly into the spotlight of the courtroom. These two figures occupy different ends of the moral spectrum, yet their methods and mindsets interlock like two sides of the same coin.

It is precisely this convergence—the strategic thinking of a criminal and the protective armor of a lawyer—that we will explore in *Criminal Mindset: Think Like a Criminal and Act Like a Lawyer*. You might flinch at the idea of learning from criminals, or you might wonder how such lessons can possibly remain ethical. Yet consider this: criminals throughout history have demonstrated a remarkable capacity for evaluating risks, exploiting opportunities, and adapting to ever-shifting conditions. They observe human behavior with predatory insight, noticing subtle tells and vulnerabilities that escape the untrained eye. Criminals understand how to slip between the cracks of a rigid system. Meanwhile, lawyers—at least the ones who thrive in their field—possess a near-surgical understanding of those same systems. They know exactly where the lines are drawn and how to maneuver near, around, or within them without stepping into ruin.

Together, these skill sets form a potent recipe for **influence**, **persuasion**, and **protection**. In the chapters to come, you will learn the predatory instincts that give criminals their edge—the meticulous observation, the calculated risk-taking, and the capacity to think several moves ahead like a grandmaster on a chessboard. You will also discover how to fortify these skills with legal literacy, ethical guardrails, and the art of building airtight defenses. When you combine the criminal's flair for the unexpected with the lawyer's comprehensive grasp of law and order, you gain a kind of "superpower": the ability to shape your own destiny with both daring creativity and prudent caution.

Yet, let us be unequivocal: *this book is not an invitation to lawlessness.* The truth is, *thinking like a criminal* does not necessarily mean *acting like one.* On the contrary, if you only adopt the predatory elements, you risk veering into realms that can sabotage your integrity, your career, and your relationships. That is why the second directive—*act like a lawyer*—is crucial. Lawyers do not rely on brute force or fear; they wield legislation, contracts, negotiations, and rhetorical finesse. When balanced correctly, these lessons teach you to move with the stealth of a thief while remaining firmly within the bounds of legality. In that sense, the synergy between the two approaches offers an unbeatable advantage: you transform yourself into a force that can never be easily outmaneuvered.

> "Power corrupts, but wisdom keeps it in check."

There is no denying the allure of power. Since the dawn of civilization, every tribe, empire, and modern society has grappled with the question: *Who holds power, and how do they keep it?* Answering that question often reveals a complex tapestry of alliances, betrayals, visions, and cunning ploys. By studying both the masterminds who operate in the shadows and the advocates who stand under the harsh lights of scrutiny, we gain a unique perspective on how power truly works. Criminals teach us *what can be done* when rules are flexible, while lawyers guide us in *what should be done* to remain legally protected.

What follows in these pages is a structured journey through the core facets of this dual mindset, beginning with a bold look at how criminals think and why they so often outsmart the very systems designed to catch them. We will delve into the primal instincts that shape their every move, the *hunt-or-be-hunted* mindset, which, when tamed, can elevate your situational awareness and strategic planning. We will stand in the dusty corners of a con artist's workshop to unmask the techniques they use to lure unsuspecting victims. We will also stroll through a courtroom to see how the brilliance of legal argumentation can reduce a seemingly airtight case to nothing but vapors. Ultimately, you will walk away seeing the world in a sharper light, ever alert to nuance and potential pitfalls, yet confident in your capacity to navigate them.

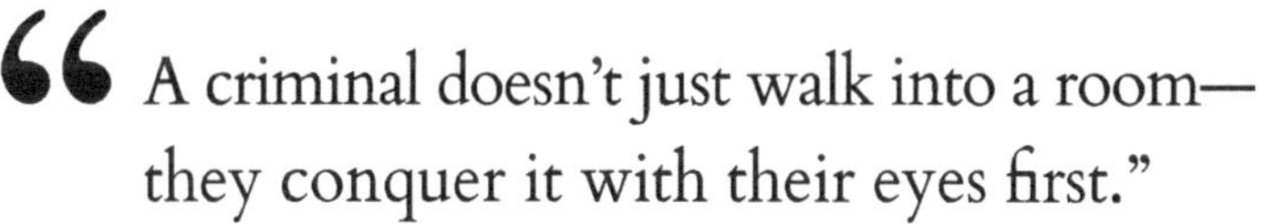

That statement underscores how everything starts with observation. Criminals, in their own transgressive way, are *students of human behavior*. If you have ever watched a skilled pickpocket in a crowded market, you know exactly what this means. Within seconds, they identify the marks—the unsuspecting tourists who wear their backpacks loosely, who fumble with their phones, whose attention is on anything but their own vulnerability. In a single fluid motion, a wallet vanishes and the pickpocket melts into the throng, leaving no trace behind. This heightened state of awareness is an invaluable asset, and it is not exclusive to criminals. Anyone can learn to observe with that same level of nuance, applying it to negotiations, business deals, or even reading the emotional undercurrent in a family gathering.

Of course, criminals do not only observe; they *exploit.* They weigh risks and rewards with a steely-eyed resolve that ordinary people seldom employ. Fear too often immobilizes honest individuals, but criminals, driven by desperation or greed, push past that barrier, trusting in their planning and audacity. Meanwhile, a skilled lawyer excels not just in spotting potential traps but in *transforming them into opportunities.* They understand how to navigate labyrinthine regulations, how to present arguments so that even unfavorable evidence can be turned into a stepping stone. When a cunning mind weds itself to a robust understanding of law, the result is a strategist who rarely sees a dead end—only new angles for approach.

The central question to keep in mind as we begin is this: *How can you ethically harness the thinking patterns of a criminal without crossing the line?* The answer lies in constantly balancing your moral compass against your hunger for achievement. It is about mastering that borderline state where you recognize how a system can be manipulated, yet you choose a path of *equitable advantage* rather than outright deceit. This is the line that the most powerful individuals in our history have walked, often discretely. Some conquer by ignoring ethics entirely.

Others fail because they insist on unwavering virtue. But those who learn to dance in the gray—those individuals transcend the usual limitations and ascend to positions of extraordinary influence.

The best criminal isn't the one who avoids getting caught—it's the one who knows how to stay within the gray areas of legality."

This insight is as true in a card game as it is in a boardroom or courtroom. Deception, after all, is not solely the domain of lawbreakers. Every day in competitive industries, CEOs and managers engage in strategic withholding of information—call it "selective honesty." Political figures carefully craft narratives that reveal certain truths while obscuring others. Even in personal relationships, people often present themselves in ways that are advantageous. The line between manipulation and influence can be *terribly* thin. Hence, the goal is not to transform you into a puppet-master who sees everyone as a mark. Instead, it is to illuminate the mental frameworks that have long given criminals an edge, so that you can incorporate their lessons in a manner that elevates your life and the lives of those around you.

When you *act like a lawyer*, you formalize your intentions with safeguards that keep your methods defensible. You adapt to laws as they evolve. You anticipate how even a seemingly benign maneuver could lead to catastrophic legal pitfalls if not executed properly. You realize the importance of paperwork, documentation, plausible deniability, and all the subtle intricacies that define a robust defense. Acting like a lawyer grants you an awareness of how to present your actions, how to negotiate terms, and how to keep your hands clean even in the most contentious of dealings. Anyone can attempt something bold, but only those who plan meticulously and legally are likely to sustain success without self-imploding.

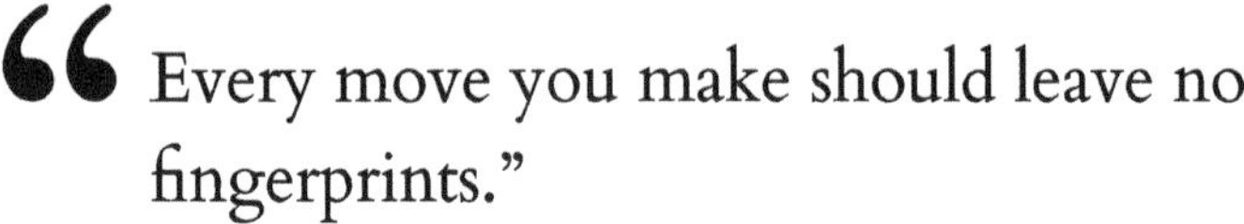

> Every move you make should leave no fingerprints."

In essence, if you can combine the unwavering confidence and opportunistic scanning of the criminal mind with the disciplined structure and foresight of the legal mind, you become unstoppable. That synergy will drive the architecture of this book. We will begin by dissecting the criminal mindset—its origins, its historical evolution, the primal instincts that feed it, and the psychological intricacies that shape every risky decision. We will then shift to the realm of law, where you will learn to see statutes not as rigid barriers but as pliable frameworks. You will discover how to *arm* yourself with legal knowledge, turning potential vulnerabilities into strongholds.

As we progress, we will explore the hustler's playbook, examining the codes criminals use to thrive undetected, and how those same principles can be harnessed ethically for personal gain. You will read stories of hustlers and cunning strategists who rose to power, only to learn how quickly that power can topple if not carefully balanced. We will talk about forging alliances—understanding how to collaborate with strong personalities without letting them overshadow you. We will also explore the art of *staying under the radar*, a skill as vital in high-stakes business negotiations as it is in covert operations.

Finally, we will confront the moral dimensions head-on. The fact is, every advantage comes with a cost. The methods taught here are no exception. Learning to observe and exploit vulnerabilities could corrupt you if you lose your ethical footing. So we will delve into the cost of power, how easily it can warp intentions, and how essential it is to guard yourself against your own darkness. Because while it is thrilling to emulate a master criminal's cunning, it is also a precarious endeavor. One misstep can destroy everything you have built.

By the end of our journey, my hope is that you will grasp a deeper truth: *we are all capable of extraordinary strategy, but it is wisdom that anchors our choices.* Rules do not have to remain unquestioned barriers; they can be gateways for innovation, provided we navigate them responsibly. And cunning need not be a synonym for evil. In fact, the most inspiring figures throughout history often displayed a remarkable knack for creative, strategic thinking—Martin Luther King Jr. used the judicial system to challenge segregation, Mahatma Gandhi leveraged the British Empire's own laws to spotlight injustice, and many leading entrepreneurs have recognized that progress often lies in reimagining the rules rather than blindly submitting to them.

> “The greatest hustler is the one who lets others believe they’re in control.”

Just as a criminal feints and misdirects so that onlookers never suspect their true intention, a skilled negotiator or leader uses subtlety and timing to guide discussions and decisions. These methods can be harnessed nobly, to uplift a community or steer a collective vision. They can also be warped by greed or selfishness. The difference, always, is in the moral compass that navigates the murky waters. This book aims to equip you with the compass, the map, and the survival skills. How you choose to employ them is entirely in your hands.

Your transformation starts here, with a willingness to step outside your comfort zone. As you turn these pages, you will learn to challenge assumptions, reinterpret obstacles, and exploit overlooked opportunities. You will discover that intimidation is not nearly as powerful as *perception* and that raw might pales in comparison to cunning deliberation. You will learn how to decipher the unspoken currents in a room, how to leverage legal knowledge to protect yourself from hidden pitfalls, and ultimately, how to craft a personal code of power that remains resilient under scrutiny.

So brace yourself for an odyssey that blends cloak-and-dagger subterfuge with the crisp enunciation of the law. Let your mind stretch in ways it perhaps never has, drawing lessons from unlikely teachers—thieves, con artists, mobsters—while steadfastly keeping your conscience in sight. Because make no mistake, *these people have perfected certain arts that can sharpen your instincts dramatically*. Yet it is the lawyer's perspective, the grand tapestry of statutes and court precedents, that allows you to refine those instincts without succumbing to chaos.

Do not be content with half-measures. A mere dabbling in these pages may spark your interest, but a committed study will spark an entirely new orientation in your thinking. If at times you feel uneasy or question the moral tightrope we walk, remember that power itself is neutral. How you harness it, how you direct its force, depends on your sense of purpose. Whether you seek to climb corporate ladders, campaign for social justice, or simply protect your family's interests, this dual mindset can serve you immensely—if used with care.

Thus, I welcome you to *Criminal Mindset: Think Like a Criminal and Act Like a Lawyer*, a journey through the labyrinth of hidden possibilities that open up when you balance primal cunning with legal discipline. May this exploration stir in you a bolder vision for what you can accomplish and, at the same time, keep you vigilant about the line between rightful ambition and destructive greed. The courthouse stands as both a symbol of justice and a fortress of secrets; let it remind you that power can be as luminous or as shadowed as you choose to make it.

We stand now on the threshold of transformation. Look around you with fresh eyes. Notice the locked doors that once seemed impassable. Glance at the people who move in your orbit—your colleagues, your rivals, your loved ones—and see them as more than static figures in an unchanging play. They are as pivotal as you in the unfolding tapestry of influence, negotiation, and hidden potential. Ready yourself, for in the chapters ahead, we shall journey deep into the art of cunning, the strength of law, and the ephemeral line that runs between them. If you are willing to learn, to unlearn, and to adapt, you may never see the world the same way again.

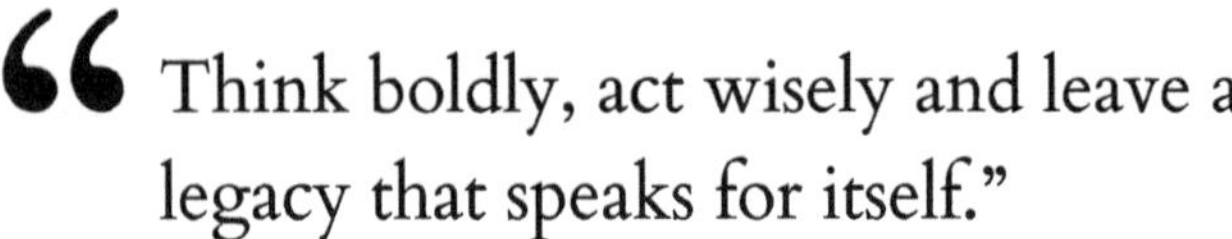

PART I

The Criminal Mindset

1
The Origins of Strategy

"The first step to power is understanding that rules exist to be bent."

It was a damp, fog-shrouded morning in Renaissance Florence when a wiry young scribe hurried through narrow cobblestone streets, clutching a worn parchment. His destination lay ahead: a nondescript wooden door with no marking other than a solitary brass knocker. Behind that door, seated at a humble oak desk, was a low-ranking official named Niccolò Machiavelli—an individual whose ideas would soon reverberate across centuries. Though Machiavelli's role in the Florentine government was modest at that time, *his mind seethed with bold notions about power, manipulation, and survival.* While the rest of the city stirred with the routine hum of merchants setting up stalls and citizens scuttling to church, Machiavelli was already penning early drafts of what would later become *The Prince*, a treatise that laid bare the uncomfortable truth that the rules of society are often more malleable than they appear.

That notion—that rules can be bent, negotiated, or even radically reimagined—has shaped the human journey from our earliest beginnings on the savannas to the present-day streets of towering metropolises. In the modern era, we witness individuals like Frank Abagnale, whose forgeries and impersonations baffled an entire airline industry. We marvel at hackers who waltz through digital security systems as though they were open doors. *All these figures, whether from the annals of history or the tabloids of today, share a single driving force: the mastery of strategy.*

But *strategy* did not begin in the polished corridors of Renaissance courts or behind the glowing screens of cyber-crooks. Its roots plunge deep into the primal instincts of our ancestors. Millennia ago, a band of early humans might have crouched in the tall grass, hearts pounding, as they observed a herd of mammoths grazing by a watering hole. Lacking the brute force to subdue such colossal beasts, these humans possessed something else: the capacity to *outthink* their prey. *Patience, observation, and precision* guided them just as they guide modern-day criminals and con artists. In those moments, when survival hinged on reading subtle shifts in the herd's formation or waiting for the perfect ambush spot, the art of strategy took its first breath.

The story of how humans learned to outmaneuver threats—both animal and human—reveals fundamental truths about the nature of power. Long before the first city-states or kingdoms rose, individual survival depended on keen awareness and the ability to orchestrate clever ruses. You might imagine the scenario: one tribe sets a trap near a riverbank while another distracts a herd from the opposite direction. This synchronization, this coordination of cunning and collaboration, became *the seed that would sprout into all advanced forms of strategy.* Centuries later, that same seed blossomed in the cunning politics of ancient courts, in the high-stakes negotiations of modern boardrooms, and, indeed, in the brazen gambits of those who live by breaking the law.

Yet the journey of strategy is not just one of bone-tipped spears and whispered conspiracies. It is equally about how societies develop laws, ethics, and codes to contain or harness the human proclivity for cunning. Think, for instance, of Hammurabi's Code in ancient Mesopotamia—a set of rules carved into stone that demanded an eye for an eye. Even as these rules sought to establish a semblance of order, clever individuals found ways around them, exploiting the ambiguous wording of decrees or forging alliances with powerful nobles who stood above common retribution. In every era, and in every community, the game of strategy has two opposing forces: *those who craft the rules and those who find ways to stretch them.*

> "Rules, in the hands of the bold, become stepping stones rather than walls."

Over time, large empires arose, each with its own tapestry of alliances, trades, and conflicts. Military strategists such as Sun Tzu in the East and Julius Caesar in the West refined the practice of warfare into a science of positioning, surprise, and deception. Look at how Sun Tzu extolled the virtues of subterfuge, advising generals to appear weak when strong and strong when weak. Or observe Caesar's deft manipulations in the Roman Senate, where he used *the law* to crush political rivals while *simultaneously* courting the public's adoration. The lesson was clear: power did not solely belong to the physically dominant, but also to the mind that could choreograph events with hidden strings.

Enter the Renaissance, a period marked by vibrant art, flourishing trade, and also the infamous cunning of Italian city-states. In Florence, Machiavelli's pen sparked controversy by suggesting that rulers should not be bound solely by moral virtue if they wished to maintain power. Even before Machiavelli gave it bold expression, the Florentine elite were no strangers to sophisticated ploys—strategic marriages that aligned fortunes, political marriages that closed rivalries, and backroom deals sealed with coded letters delivered under cover of night. Machiavelli simply pulled back the curtain, unveiling for all the world the mechanics of influence operating underneath civility. To some, his words were sacrilege; to others, they were an indispensable guide to navigating the treacherous waters of human ambition.

But the Renaissance was only one crescendo in an ongoing symphony of power plays. As human society advanced into the era of industrialization, new fronts for strategy emerged: corporate competition, global finance, and eventually, the digital realm. Industrial titans like John D. Rockefeller cornered markets with ruthless efficiency. Innovative magnates like Andrew Carnegie leveraged steel production and wage negotiations in ways that forced entire industries to dance to their tune. If you peel back the layers of those so-called "legitimate" successes, you find an undercurrent of cunning reminiscent of ancient hunts—covert alliances, market manipulation, and carefully orchestrated illusions of scarcity or abundance. Where law and ethics drew lines, these magnates learned to walk right up to the boundary, sometimes dipping a toe over, then pulling back before accusations could harden into legal action.

> "Human progress is the story of cunning wrapped in evolving forms of morality."

Now, let us turn our gaze to a different branch of strategy, one that glides through the shadows rather than shining in the corporate limelight. Modern con artists, hackers, and thieves achieve their goals with surgical precision, exploiting gaps in our understanding of technology, bureaucracy, or social norms. Consider Frank Abagnale *(Catch Me If You Can)*, who faked credentials to pilot planes, practice law, and doctor medical charts—all by harnessing the same cunning that ancient hunters once used to ambush prey. His achievements were not feats of brute force but of psychological insight. He recognized that *a uniform, a confident stride, and the right jargon* could open doors most people never even dared to knock on.

If the Renaissance taught us that appearances could be meticulously crafted to influence perception, Abagnale proved that the principle still thrives in the modern age.

But why do so many criminals—and even top-tier negotiators—succeed where others flounder? Part of the answer lies in *understanding the invisible levers that move a person or system.* That includes fear, greed, pride, and the reluctance most people have to challenge an authority figure—or someone who simply appears to be an authority figure. When leveraged properly, these human tendencies become instruments of control. Many are the times that a slip of the tongue, a casual remark, or a standard operating procedure has opened a gaping vulnerability for a shrewd strategist.

All too often, people imagine criminals as reckless individuals too impulsive to follow social norms. In truth, *effective criminals are among the most methodical humans on the planet.* They plan meticulously, exploit small oversights, and protect themselves with a veil of plausible deniability. Some criminals manage to operate for years without detection precisely because they have studied the legalities that govern their territory. They know how to appear harmless or even beneficial to those who might otherwise suspect wrongdoing.

The twist here—and the central theme of this entire book—is that *the same skills that make a thief successful can also help you succeed in entirely lawful pursuits.* The difference lies in how you use these abilities. A thief sees a locked door and wonders how to pick it. A lawyer sees a locked door and asks if they hold the legal key.

Someone who can harness both perspectives sees a world not of barriers but of *endless possibilities*, each door an opportunity waiting to be explored, often with full permission, but occasionally by pushing against the edges of what is considered permissible.

We arrive, then, at a bold proposition: *What if you could harness the raw, adaptive brilliance of a criminal's mindset and channel it through the robust framework of the law?* This synergy is what sets truly formidable individuals apart. They are neither naive do-gooders nor reckless renegades. Rather, they are students of strategy who respect the power of law but also appreciate the infinite ways in which rules can be worked to one's advantage. In a world where laws can exceed thousands of pages, where corporate regulations tie up entire legal teams for years, and where social norms shift with each new technological wave, it is those who *understand the fluidity of boundaries* who remain on top.

Society does not crumble because of cunning; it evolves because cunning reveals where old rules have grown obsolete."

If there is one constant across eras—from prehistoric hunts to the digital leaps of the twenty-first century—it is that strategy abhors stagnation. The greatest legal minds know that laws are forever being tested, amended, and reinterpreted. The most ingenious criminals sense that no system, no matter how rigid, is entirely foolproof.

Wars have been won and lost by cunning alone, without the loud clash of swords or the thunder of artillery. In the same vein, business empires have risen or fallen through a single stroke of strategic brilliance or oversight. That is the sweet spot where cunning meets structure, and it is also the underlying current of *Criminal Mindset: Think Like a Criminal and Act Like a Lawyer.*

Of course, *acting like a lawyer* means more than simply *staying* on the right side of the law. It involves cultivating a nuanced perception of how laws are formed, how they are enforced, and how they can be interpreted. Law is a complex tapestry of precedents, interpretations, and cultural mores. To navigate it effectively, you must read between the lines just as carefully as a con artist reads body language. Senior advocates do not merely memorize laws; they *live* them, constantly watching for the slightest shift in the legal landscape that can open new pathways or close old ones. Once you pair that finesse with the criminal's willingness to test the cracks in any structure, you awaken to a world of strategic possibility.

Look again at Machiavelli. Many interpret his famous line—*"It is better to be feared than loved, if you cannot be both"*—as a dark prescription for ruthless leadership. Yet at its core, Machiavelli's entire philosophy was an acknowledgment that *power is fluid.* He saw how rulers who clung to moral absolutism were often devoured by those more flexible in their methods. He also noted that a ruler who betrays the public trust too severely, or who fails to mask their manipulations, inevitably faces rebellion. Balance, for Machiavelli, was paramount: you bend rules, but you cannot shatter them beyond repair lest you trigger the wrath of forces you cannot control.

In many respects, the *criminal-lawmaker* dichotomy is a modern echo of that same caution. A seasoned criminal studies law not to destroy it utterly, but to exploit it selectively. A seasoned lawyer understands that upholding the law does not necessarily mean ignoring its gray areas. The synergy between these perspectives can be remarkably powerful, but it must also be approached with care, because illusions of grandeur can blind even the sharpest strategist. Consider how many infamous leaders in world history have fallen prey to their own hubris, believing themselves untouchable until reality collapsed on them with scandal or rebellion.

> Cunning is a sharp blade; it can carve a path to glory or cut its wielder down in a single misstep."

To harness cunning for constructive ends, you must *recognize* its dangers. One danger is losing sight of ethics, drifting into moral compromise that may eventually devour your reputation and peace of mind. Another danger is underestimating the power of law itself, which, when wielded by equally cunning adversaries, can entangle you in lawsuits, prosecutions, or social condemnation. Even Machiavelli warned that a prince who relies too heavily on deceit may ignite fearsome opposition. The key is to walk a fine line: to see rules for the tools they are, but also to remember that too much tampering will provoke a backlash you might not survive.

Therein lies the brilliance of combining criminal intuition with legal discipline. Strategy becomes more than a game of hide-and-seek with the authorities or an endless scramble to close legal loopholes. It evolves into a calculated art form wherein each move is predicated on a deep understanding of human nature and the frameworks that govern it. The best criminals demonstrate how far creativity can stretch the boundaries. The best lawyers demonstrate how to safely navigate and sometimes *expand* those boundaries from within. When these two intelligences meet, you learn to look at a seemingly locked gate and ask two questions in tandem: *How can I break in?* and *Is there a legitimate way to open it?*

The answer to both questions might be the same technique—just applied with different intentions. A forger might replicate signatures to steal funds, while a savvy lawyer might replicate documents to *verify* or *expose* a financial imbalance during a trial. Both use the skill of duplication, but one does so covertly to violate trust, while the other does so openly to restore it. The difference is purpose, governed by an ethical framework or the lack thereof.

Only the strategist who understands the entire spectrum—from darkness to light—can truly call themselves a master."

That is why *Chapter 1: The Origins of Strategy* is more than a historical overview. It is an invitation to see how the primal survival impulse of our ancestors evolved into grand tactics of warfare, politics, finance, and crime. We study Machiavelli not to become ruthless, but to appreciate the necessity of flexibility. We examine con artists like Abagnale not to celebrate deceit, but to glean the power of reading social signals and systems. Through it all, we keep coming back to that fundamental concept: *rules exist to be bent*, because they are designed by fallible humans responding to ever-changing conditions.

Yet it is also vital to acknowledge that bending rules without moral or legal anchor can lead to chaos or personal ruin. Just as a lion in the savanna risks a fatal kick if it attacks a well-defended buffalo head-on, a person who underestimates the wrath of law or the moral outrage of the public may find themselves swiftly undone. Strategy, in its purest sense, is *neither ethical nor unethical*; it is simply the capacity to forge a path under constraints. *You supply the ethics.* You decide whether that path leads to honorable success or destructive greed.

As you venture forward in this book, keep this foundational lesson close to heart. Strategy is ancient, adaptive, and omnipresent. Whether you are eyeing a better position at work, negotiating a lease, or confronting the labyrinthine puzzle of life's unexpected challenges, the roots of strategic thinking lie in the same primal soil that once guided spear-wielding hunters and Machiavellian princes alike. The difference lies in how you choose to employ it, and that is where acting like a lawyer becomes crucial.

From here, our exploration will deepen. We will move from these broad historical strokes into the specifics of what it means to *think like a criminal* in contemporary settings. We will dissect the *predator's mindset*, unearthing how criminals train their senses to pick apart weaknesses in people and systems. Then, we will pivot to the rigorous discipline of the law, discovering how knowledge of legal frameworks can shield you from catastrophic missteps. Finally, we will fuse these components into a cohesive approach that arms you with not only the will to dominate your field but also the wisdom to do so ethically and sustainably.

All that begins with appreciating what this first chapter has laid out: *strategy is as old as conflict itself.* It does not care whether you wear a crown or a disguise, whether you argue from behind a judge's bench or in an alleyway with forged credentials in your pocket. Strategy simply *is*, an ever-present current in the human experience, guiding us toward victory—or downfall—depending on how adeptly we wield it.

When you are ready to take that next step, remember Machiavelli's lesson: *political or personal triumphs rarely happen by accident; they happen because someone sees through the façade of fixed rules and seizes the fluid space where opportunity dwells.* Let that knowledge sharpen your instincts, and let the chapters ahead mold your capabilities. The moment you embrace the truth that rules can be bent, you realize just how boundless the horizon of possibility really is. And in that realization lies the seed of true power.

Prepare yourself, for in the following chapter, we will enter the realm of predatory thinking. We will watch how criminals size up a room, a system, or a human target with an intensity that can be both astonishing and unsettling. Even if you never choose to break a single law in your life, learning how *others* do it—how they spot weaknesses, set traps, and orchestrate illusions—will expand your vision. You will no longer be just another face in the crowd. You will become the observer, the analyst, the *strategist*. In that transformation, the wisdom of the ages merges with your own unique perspective, and the result is a power that can shape not just your fate, but the fate of those around you.

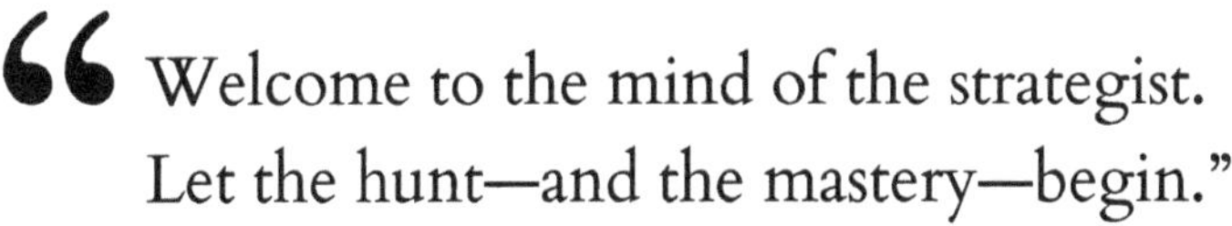

2

Thinking Like a Predator

> "A predator doesn't merely look at the world; it dissects it, piece by piece."

The late-night casino lights shimmered across the bustling main floor, illuminating faces full of optimism and anxiety. Gamblers clutched their chips as they stared at the roulette wheel or the flop of a poker hand, each person convinced they had a method, a strategy, or perhaps even a stroke of luck that would tilt the odds in their favor. Amid the flurry of voices, clinking glassware, and the mechanical chime of slot machines, a lone figure hovered near one of the blackjack tables. At first glance, this individual seemed no different from the other casino guests. They sipped a drink, laughed politely at the dealer's jokes, and occasionally placed modest bets.

But if you paid attention to their eyes, you would notice something *altogether different* happening. They were watching, *always* watching—every flicker of tension in another player's face, every slight hesitation in the dealer's routine, every small gesture that betrayed how a person felt about their cards.

That individual, unbeknownst to everyone around them, was operating in *predator mode*. In that moment, they were not just playing a card game; they were hunting. The currency was chips, but the stakes were far deeper. Any sign of weakness on the part of another player was an invitation to press an advantage. Any unpredictable move by the house was quickly analyzed for a possible exploit. Patience, observation, and precision formed the unholy trinity of this predator's mindset. They sat quietly, confident in their ability to anticipate *where* and *when* to strike.

In many ways, criminal masterminds operate like this in every situation they encounter, not just in a casino. They do not rely on blind luck. Instead, they observe with laser focus, waiting for the perfect moment to act. This chapter delves into that *predator's perspective*, offering you a glimpse of how criminals train their senses to detect vulnerabilities and seize opportunities. While we do not condone breaking the law, understanding this mindset can give you a potent edge in virtually any competitive environment, from job interviews to corporate boardrooms. If a negotiation is a battlefield, then the party who thinks like a predator is the one who often dictates the terms of engagement.

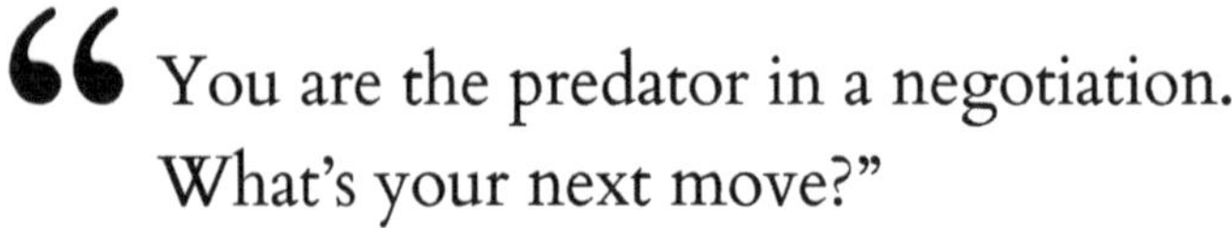

“You are the predator in a negotiation. What’s your next move?”

That question might make you pause. It should. In most of life’s dealings, we imagine ourselves as innocents hoping for a fair exchange. Yet from the predator’s viewpoint, any negotiation is a strategic hunt. You do not walk into the room simply to speak your piece; you enter armed with a wealth of knowledge about the opposition. You quietly evaluate how they sit, how they breathe, whether their gaze flickers nervously, how their voice quivers when they sense a disadvantage. You note these details like a hawk circling overhead, choosing the moment to swoop down for maximum effect.

In *every* negotiation, someone holds the upper hand. It can be an employer meeting a potential hire, a homeowner discussing renovation quotes with a contractor, or a multinational corporation bargaining for a merger. The question is: **Will you be the one who subtly influences the outcome, or will you be the one who gets cornered?** Predators never settle for the latter. They devote themselves to studying the environment until they understand exactly how to gain the upper hand.

Consider a real-world example in Frank Abagnale, the con artist made famous by the film *Catch Me If You Can*. Abagnale, at a shockingly young age, impersonated pilots, doctors, and even lawyers. He did so not through brute force or high technology, but through an uncanny talent for reading people and situations. He understood precisely how individuals in positions of authority behaved and *mirrored* them with impeccable detail—right down to body language, tone of voice, and the subtle dynamic of social hierarchies. By carefully studying how a pilot spoke to flight attendants or how a doctor carried himself around nurses and patients, Abagnale assumed those roles convincingly. He noticed minuscule discrepancies in the way people responded to authority, exploited those discrepancies, and slipped effortlessly into roles that should have been impossible for a stranger to fill.

That is *predatory thinking* in action: searching not just for cracks in a system, but also for emotional and social blind spots in the people who operate that system. A criminal sees an organization as a living, breathing entity, complete with routines, habits, moods, and interpersonal relationships. A predator assesses which parts of that entity are vulnerable and then strikes with precision.

Yet, you do not have to break the law to tap into this perspective. A savvy entrepreneur exhibits similar thinking when scouting potential partnerships and analyzing market gaps. They scrutinize the competition's weakest points, noticing unserved customer needs or overlooked technological innovations. They lie in wait until the competition grows complacent, then launch a product or strategy that capitalizes on those *unseen* market niches.

In the same vein, a skilled attorney applies predator-like focus in the courtroom. They listen intently for inconsistent testimony, watch the jury's reactions with unwavering attention, and wait for precisely the right moment to deliver a damning question that unravels the opposing counsel's argument. To onlookers, it may appear that the attorney simply stumbled upon a "gotcha" moment, but in reality, that moment is often the result of painstaking observation, strategic timing, and a willingness to exploit the other side's lapses.

Patience, Observation, and Precision

These are the pillars of thinking like a predator. Remove any one of them, and the structure collapses. Patience means resisting the temptation to lunge at every hint of advantage. It means allowing the environment to reveal *its* vulnerabilities, letting people become comfortable enough to lower their guard. Observation is the lens through which you gather intelligence: reading faces, noticing how individuals interact, spotting patterns in behaviors, and identifying who holds influence in a given setting. Precision is the execution of your plan at the exact moment it will have the greatest effect.

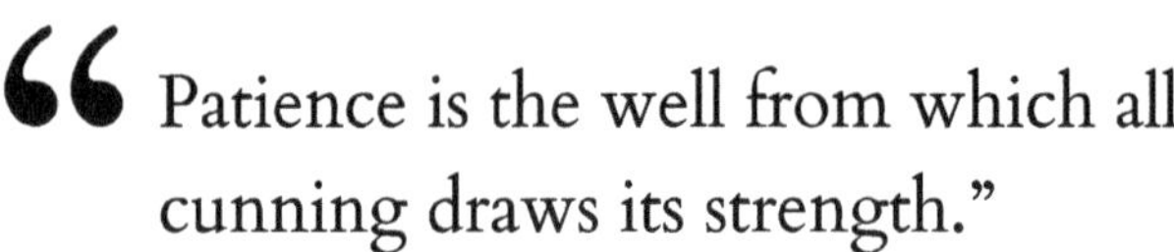

A predator who lacks patience is like a fisherman casting his net too soon. He might catch a few small fish, but he will miss the opportunity to snare the prize that swims deeper, closer to the perfect moment. Watch how a lion hunts in the wild. The lion does not sprint aimlessly into a herd of zebras. It crouches low in the tall grass, muscles taut, every sense awake, waiting for the right target to drift from the herd. Only then does the lion pounce, unleashing its power when the prey's escape routes are fewest.

In a high-stakes negotiation, patience manifests as the ability to let the other side reveal their positions and fears. You do not rush in with demands or concessions. You wait, you read the small tells, and you encourage them to speak until they've inadvertently shown you where their weaknesses lie.

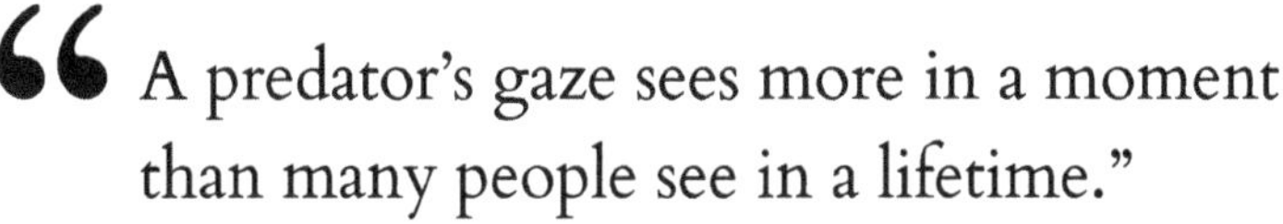

Observation, the second pillar, might be the most critical. Without accurate intelligence, no plan—however cunning—will succeed. Criminals often excel at observation because their freedom depends on it. A single moment of inattentiveness could lead to capture or betrayal. Consequently, they train themselves to read micro-expressions, shifts in posture, fluctuations in voice pitch, and patterns in daily routines. They *know* that human beings operate like clockwork in many aspects of life. If you track those rhythms, you can slip through security gaps that no one else noticed.

Consider a classic scenario: a well-prepared thief scouting a mansion before attempting a burglary. They do not simply barge in at random. First, they may take note of the gardener's schedule, the maid's usual vacuuming routine, and the homeowner's typical lunch outings.

They realize that *even the most thorough security system relies on human oversight*. Perhaps the gardener always leaves a side gate ajar on Tuesdays. Maybe the homeowner forgets to lock the back window when stepping out to run errands. Armed with such knowledge, the thief pinpoints the perfect moment to make their move.

Similarly, in everyday life, you can harness this keen power of observation to spot opportunities for career advancement, sense unspoken tensions in a group, or identify the hidden agenda in a business deal. Once you see the patterns, you can position yourself to strike—or to retreat—at the most beneficial moment.

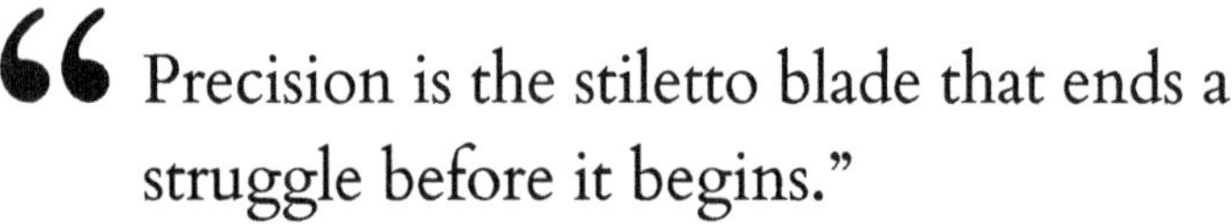

Precision, the final pillar, is the art of hitting your target with minimal wasted effort. Some might call it *timing*, others might call it *calculated risk*. Whatever the term, it involves a near-instinctual sense of *when* to commit. In business, it might mean launching a product when a rival is distracted by internal problems. In a relationship, it could be bringing up a sensitive topic when the other person is most receptive. In a courtroom, it is the deciding question that unravels a witness's credibility.

Criminals often demonstrate this kind of precision in the execution of a heist. After months of reconnaissance, they might choose an hour when law enforcement is shift-changing or a holiday weekend when banks have minimal staff. They do not waste energy on unnecessary theatrics. They strike exactly at the nerve point.

The lawful equivalent might be a strategic investor who waits until stock prices dip to their lowest—perhaps spurred by fleeting bad press—then buys heavily before the market rebounds. Everyone else sees gloom and panic, but the strategic investor sees an opening. Then, once the market recovers, they profit enormously because they had the resolve to strike precisely when others hesitated.

Negotiation as a Hunt

Imagine you are about to enter a tense business negotiation. The stakes are high. A major contract worth crores is on the table, and you have to secure it for your firm. The opposing party is a seasoned negotiator with a reputation for aggression and intimidation. Most people in your shoes would walk in with an immediate sense of dread or confrontation, feeling compelled to prove their worthiness from the outset. But you, thinking like a predator, do the opposite.

You arrive early, well before the meeting begins. You calmly greet the receptionist, make a friendly remark about the day's events, and study the environment while pretending to be casually checking your phone. Is the opposing party rushing in at the last minute? Does the negotiator appear nervous, tapping a pen or shuffling papers excessively? Are there indicators that they're juggling too many meetings at once, thus prone to oversight? You store each small observation in your mental filing cabinet.

Then, once you finally take your seat across the table, you do not talk first. You wait. You *listen.* You let them attempt their intimidation tactics. You watch how they speak. If they are prone to raising their voice when they feel cornered, note it. If they fidget with their tie when challenged, note that as well. You remain outwardly calm, asking innocuous questions that encourage them to reveal what truly matters to them in this deal. Are they time-pressured because of another looming deadline? Are they more concerned about preserving their company's public image than about maximizing profit? Every snippet of information becomes a potential point of leverage.

With patience, observation, and precision guiding you, you know exactly when to present your first concession. Perhaps you give ground on a minor clause that signals goodwill. The negotiator, sensing a small victory, becomes more confident and starts talking more openly. At last, you detect the exact moment to spring your main ask—when they seem eager to finalize details to claim a quick "win." In that critical sliver of time, you deliver your demands with unflinching clarity. Because they are off-balance and anxious to close, they yield on key points. The deal is sealed in your favor.

Bridging Instinct with Ethic

One might question the morality of adopting a predator's mindset, but keep in mind that *predatory awareness* does not require you to become exploitative or cruel. It merely shifts your focus to a heightened level of strategy. You remain free to apply your moral compass to decide when and how to strike. A wise predator does not tear apart the herd indiscriminately; they select their moment in alignment with a core objective. If your objective is *ethical success*, then thinking like a predator need not lead you astray. It will merely empower you with sharper instincts and a readiness to seize opportunities that others might overlook.

Consider, too, that many injustices have been rectified by individuals who possessed this very trait. Social activists, whistleblowers, and investigative journalists often display predatory focus in their pursuits. They patiently gather evidence, observe the patterns of wrongdoing, and strike at the precise moment when their revelations can have the greatest societal impact. Their moral cause remains noble, yet their methods share similarities with how a thief studies the vulnerability of a vault. The difference lies in their intention and the outcome they aim to achieve.

How to Begin Training Your Predator Mind

If you are curious about how to develop this heightened perspective, start by simply *watching*—and do so more deeply than usual. Set aside a week to become hyper-aware of your surroundings. When you enter a café, notice the layout, the staff's routines, the mood of other patrons. Observe how the barista greets each customer—do they display genuine warmth, or is it a forced politeness that cracks under stress? In your workplace, note who speaks first in meetings, who dominates the conversation, who remains silent but clearly attentive, and who is bored or daydreaming.

Your goal in this phase is not to judge or intervene. It is merely to gather data, to see with fresh eyes how other humans *truly operate* when they think nobody is watching. Over time, this practice of heightened observation will become second nature. You will naturally begin to piece together patterns and anticipate outcomes. You will develop a sense of timing that aligns with the flow of your environment, much like a hunter attuned to the rustling of leaves or the snapping of a twig.

From there, your sense of precision grows. In a conversation, you will sense the perfect instant to introduce a difficult topic, knowing you have the other person's full attention. In negotiations, you will read the signals of discomfort or eagerness that flash across the other party's face, and you will tailor your approach accordingly. Even in friendships and family settings, you may notice how small gestures or repeated phrases can hint at deeper needs or unspoken tensions. Suddenly, the world seems rife with hidden cues you never noticed before.

The hunt is not about cruelty, but about clarity of purpose."

This is where you begin to merge the predator's mindset with the ethical framework of a disciplined professional. A predator's thinking is ultimately about clarity—knowing exactly what you want and understanding precisely how you might obtain it. Channel that clarity into pursuits that enrich your life and the lives of those around you rather than plunging into questionable moral territory.

Still, a word of caution: once you taste the power of heightened awareness and strategic timing, it can become tempting to manipulate situations purely for personal gain, ignoring the consequences for others. This is the slippery slope that criminals slide down. Left unchecked by a moral compass, the predator's mindset can evolve into a darker pattern of exploitation. That is why the next phases of our journey will address how to anchor these predatory instincts in an ethical and legal framework—*to think like a criminal without becoming one*, to harness cunning in ways that align with lawful boundaries, and to cultivate a moral backbone that stands firm even when the allure of easy advantage beckons.

Because the truth is, you do not want to be the hunted. Whether in business, relationships, or life's countless unspoken contests, those who drift passively often become the prey. They walk into ambushes they never see coming: a manipulative co-worker undermines them, a partner silently resents them, a competitor seizes a market they believed was secure. Thinking like a predator ensures that you remain *one step ahead*. It heightens your senses, primes you for decisive action, and arms you with the knowledge that no detail is too small when a true opportunity or threat lurks in your midst.

Remember that the path of power is lined with pitfalls. The skills you develop here are double-edged blades, and wielding them carelessly can cut deeply. Yet in the hands of a disciplined mind, these same skills become the keys to unlocking levels of influence, success, and self-assurance that few ever attain. With each chapter, we will add layers to this understanding, culminating in a synergy of criminal acumen and legal safeguard. You will not just know how to plot a course; you will understand how to defend that course against all challenges.

For now, let the seed of predatory thinking take root. Notice how your daily interactions shift as you become more vigilant, more patiently attuned to others, and more precise in your actions. Revel in the sensation of seeing angles you once missed, the small but telling changes in tone or body language that betray someone's hidden motive. In time, these observations will meld seamlessly into your daily rhythm, and you will move through life with the quiet assurance of a hunter who knows every inch of their domain.

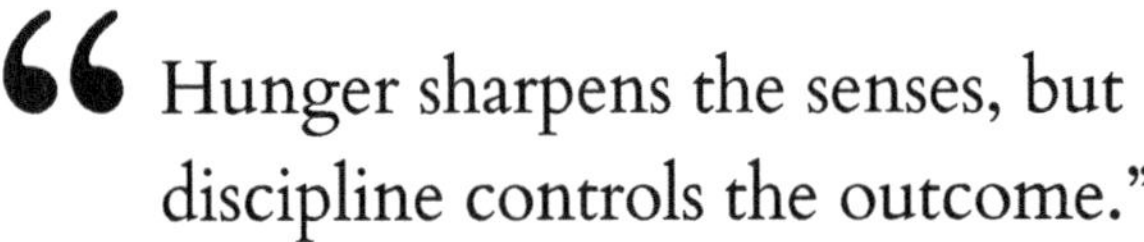

Keep that phrase in mind as you progress. Hunger fuels the predator's focus, but discipline—and soon, the knowledge of how the law operates—will be the force that keeps you from straying into self-destruction. The next chapter will deepen our exploration of how criminals absorb and analyze their environments, moving beyond mere observation to the art of reading an entire *room.* Prepare yourself, for once you master that skill, no room will ever truly be off-limits, and no conversation will unfold without your awareness of its deeper currents.

Remember: *thinking like a predator* is not a question of morality; it is a question of *capability*. Morality comes into play when you decide how to wield that newfound power. So hone your skills, remain vigilant, and brace for the next step of your transformation. The hunt has only just begun, and your eyes are finally beginning to open.

3
Reading the Room

> "A criminal doesn't just walk into a room—they conquer it with their eyes first."

There was a faint hum of hushed chatter in the crowded art gallery, punctuated by the clink of champagne glasses and polite laughter. Soft spotlights illuminated the paintings on the walls, each masterpiece vying for the admiration of the well-heeled patrons drifting from piece to piece. Despite the serene setting, the energy in the room was electric. Seasoned collectors sized up the competition with practiced smiles, each silently hoping to secure the night's most coveted acquisition.

Standing near the gallery entrance was a woman with an elegant black shawl draped across her shoulders. At first glance, she appeared to be just another affluent visitor, perhaps a socialite or art connoisseur. But if you watched her closely, you might notice that her gaze lingered less on the canvases and more on the people admiring them. She observed the way the gallery owner flitted nervously between important guests, how an eager journalist tried to pin down interviews and the subtle manner in which certain collectors gravitated toward specific styles of art. Through it all, she maintained a relaxed smile. No one suspected that she was anything other than a polite onlooker.

Yet in her mind, she was working through a meticulously crafted plan. If you could peer behind her composed demeanor, you'd find a criminal's mind racing to identify who was distracted, who was carrying valuables, and which corners of the gallery lacked security cameras. She was *reading the room* in a way that few others ever do—scanning for vulnerability, analyzing body language, pinpointing pivotal social hierarchies. To a skilled observer like her, the artwork was merely a backdrop. *People* were the true canvas on display.

In this chapter, we delve into the *art of reading a room*, a skill that transcends any single context. Criminals, by the nature of their high-stakes existence, have honed an almost uncanny ability to gauge environments and personalities within seconds. They must do so to avoid detection, to pick optimal targets, and to maximize their chances of escape. Yet the same skill set can be used productively—and ethically—in everyday life. Whether you're delivering a presentation at work, meeting potential clients, or stepping into a lively family gathering, your capacity to read people and surroundings will determine how effectively you navigate the unfolding dynamics.

Think of it this way: most people walk into a room and immediately become absorbed by their own insecurities or immediate objectives. They fail to notice the subtle shift in someone's posture, or the sudden tension in the air when a particular topic arises. In contrast, the *criminal mind* is attuned to **every flicker** of body language, every hushed remark, every stray glance that could hint at conflict or opportunity. This heightened level of awareness can be taught and practiced. It demands that you suspend your assumptions and *truly observe* the social theater unfolding around you.

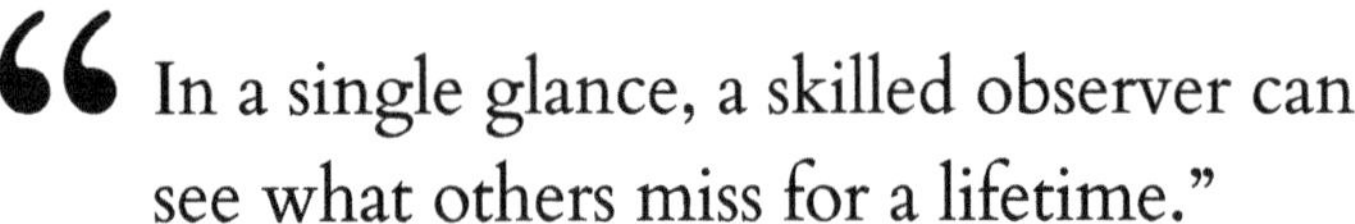

> "In a single glance, a skilled observer can see what others miss for a lifetime."

When we talk about *reading the room*, we're not discussing a casual, half-hearted survey. We mean the deliberate act of dissecting an environment to understand its power dynamics, alliances, and vulnerabilities. Think of a lion emerging onto a savanna: before making a move, the lion scans the herd, identifies the weakest or most accessible prey, and plots its approach. While we may not be prowling through tall grass in search of dinner, we *are* often navigating competitive or emotionally charged spaces where a single misstep can jeopardize our goals.

For criminals, this scanning process is a matter of survival. One wrong move, one overlooked camera, one misread security guard, and they face incarceration—or worse. Thus, criminals learn to be *hyper-vigilant*. They walk into a building and immediately note potential exit points, the number of staff on duty, the approximate location of security personnel, and even the general mood or morale of employees. If tensions are high among the staff, a clever criminal might exploit that friction to go unnoticed. Conversely, if everyone is relaxed and sociable, that might pose different risks and opportunities.

In our daily lives, we often neglect such scanning because we feel relatively safe or because we assume that social norms will protect us. But if you *train yourself* to read a room with criminal-level acuity—while adhering to ethical guidelines—you gain an enormous advantage. You'll pick up on who is the decision-maker in a business meeting, who might be harboring hidden doubts, or who is quietly evaluating your every word. Armed with these insights, you can adapt your approach to strengthen alliances, correct misunderstandings before they harden, and defuse hostility before it escalates.

"The face says more in a fraction of a second than words can manage in hours."

The criminal mind pays special attention to *micro-expressions*—fleeting facial cues that betray a person's true feelings before they have time to conceal them. For example, the corners of someone's mouth might tighten ever so slightly when they hear a rival's name, or their eyebrows might lift just a fraction when they're both surprised and intrigued. These micro-expressions are not always easy to spot because they last less than a second. Yet they reveal powerful clues about *how people really feel*, even when their words say otherwise.

A skilled poker player or con artist often capitalizes on this knowledge by wearing a mask of neutrality while diligently scanning opponents' faces for any twitch or grimace. In a negotiation, noticing a brief flash of worry could mean the other party fears losing the deal more than they let on—information you can use to your advantage. Similarly, detecting a momentary spark of excitement could signal that you've hit upon a topic they're passionate about, giving you a pathway to secure common ground.

But micro-expressions are not just for con artists and gamblers. The next time you're in a tense meeting or a family discussion, observe the faces around you carefully. Notice how quickly expressions change when certain subjects arise. Look for the flicker of annoyance, the fleeting grin of satisfaction, or the brief narrowing of eyes that screams *resentment*. Once you see these signs, you're able to tailor your responses far more effectively than someone who moves through conversations blindly, missing the silent language at play.

The Posture of Truth

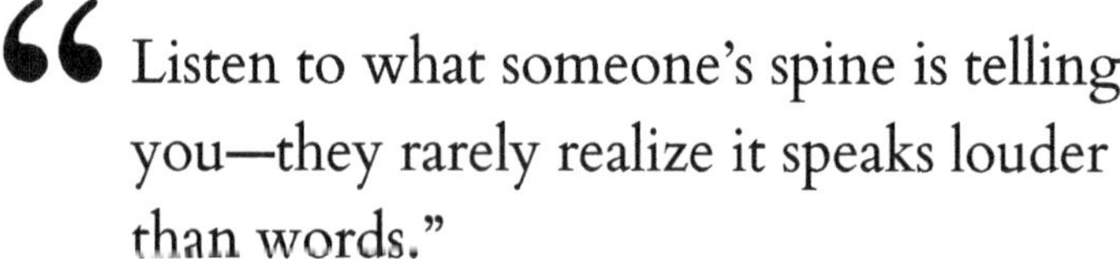

> "Listen to what someone's spine is telling you—they rarely realize it speaks louder than words."

If faces tell half the story, *body language* narrates the rest. A person's posture, the angle of their feet, the tension in their shoulders, and even the way they breathe can all communicate underlying emotions or intentions. Criminals analyze body language not just because it helps them pick out the best potential marks, but also because it can alert them to *danger.* A security guard standing stiffly with clenched fists and a locked jaw is a far greater threat than a guard who's slouching and scrolling through a phone.

For instance, if someone angles their torso or feet away from you during a conversation, it may imply they're disinterested or itching to leave. If they keep their arms crossed while subtly leaning back, they might be feeling defensive or protective of their space. Conversely, open palms and a forward-leaning posture usually signal that someone is receptive to what you're saying.

Criminals—particularly con artists—often use deliberate body language to establish trust. They know that maintaining eye contact at the right intervals, mirroring the other person's gestures, and standing or sitting in a relaxed yet open manner can lower suspicions. They understand that *people respond not just to words, but to the entire package of verbal and nonverbal cues.*

The takeaway for law-abiding individuals is that when you're entering a critical conversation—be it a job interview, a sales pitch, or even a heart-to-heart talk with a loved one—your body language should be as deliberate as your words. Show receptiveness by uncrossing your arms and leaning slightly forward. Convey calm confidence by keeping your chin level and your shoulders relaxed. This conscious deployment of body language can help you guide interactions in a more positive and fruitful direction.

Tapping into Patterns

Habit betrays us all—learn someone's pattern, and you learn their vulnerability."

Beyond micro-expressions and posture lies the broader realm of *behavioral cues*, the day-to-day habits people form, often without noticing. Criminals thrive on these patterns because *what is predictable can be exploited.* That might mean figuring out that an executive checks their voicemail every evening at exactly six o'clock, leaving a few critical minutes when their assistant's desk is unattended. Or discovering that a wealthy homeowner never sets the alarm after taking the dog out for a late-night walk.

However, these behavioral patterns are not limited to criminal targets. In a social or professional context, people also exhibit dependable routines: the coworker who always arrives early to snag coffee, the manager who never answers emails in the afternoon, the friend who always cancels plans on short notice because they're overcommitted. By taking note of these habits, you can *anticipate challenges and opportunities.* If your manager never responds to afternoon messages, you can time your important requests for the morning when they're most receptive. If your friend often cancels evening plans, you might schedule your get-together for a lunch break, improving the odds they'll actually show up.

From the criminal perspective, these patterns are vulnerabilities—open windows to slip through. From the ethical perspective, they are stepping stones to more effective communication and planning. Recognizing that people are creatures of habit can help you coordinate tasks, preempt obstacles, and build rapport by aligning your schedule with theirs when possible.

The Conqueror's Stance

Confidence disarms suspicion—master your entrance, and half the battle is won."

One of the most fundamental lessons criminals internalize is how to *enter a room* in a manner that aligns with their goals. If they need to stay invisible, they'll slip in quietly, avoid direct eye contact, and blend into the background. If they need to assert authority or appear important, they might stride in with a purposeful gait, meet people's gazes, and speak in commanding tones. *Every element of the entrance is calibrated.*

Even in legitimate business or social settings, the way you enter a space can set the tone for everything that follows. Step in with hesitant movements, eyes locked on the ground, and you might project insecurity—inviting more dominant personalities to overshadow you. Walk in with an arrogant swagger, and you might kindle defensiveness or resentment. *Aim instead for calm assurance.* Keep your head level, your posture upright, and allow a brief moment to survey the room, acknowledging those present without seeming intrusive. This approach strikes a balance that can instantly convey respect for the environment and a quiet sense of self-assurance.

Criminals often call this *the conqueror's stance*, a posture that signals to onlookers that *you belong* in that space. Consider the infamous heists where thieves posed as electricians, repair crews, or catering staff. They navigated restricted areas without raising an eyebrow precisely because their demeanor and stance indicated they had every right to be there. If you can master that kind of *poise*, you'll find yourself more capable of commanding respect in boardrooms, conferences, and social gatherings—even when surrounded by influential or intimidating figures.

Engaging with Silence

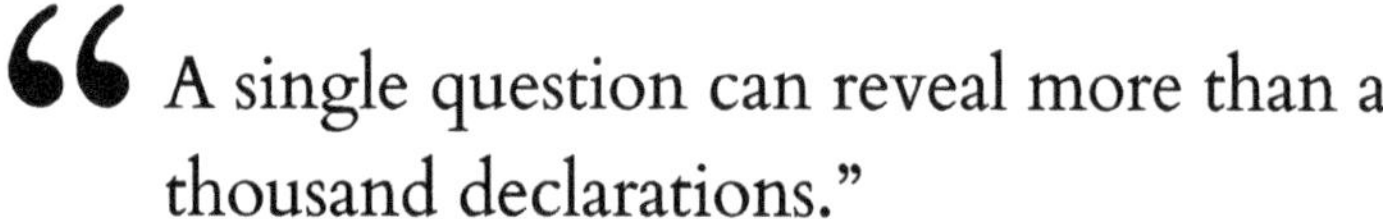

Criminals, especially those well-versed in social engineering, understand the *power of silence.* They know that an awkward pause often compels others to fill the gap by volunteering information they might otherwise withhold. In many interrogations or negotiations, the one who can *endure silence* gains the upper hand.

Try this in your own interactions: the next time someone finishes speaking, resist the urge to immediately reply. Let a few seconds pass. Watch how they react. Do they fidget? Do they offer additional details to justify their stance? Silence can be disconcerting, prompting others to reveal more than they intend. In tense settings—like a salary negotiation or a heated discussion—a carefully deployed silence can steer the conversation in your favor.

Moreover, criminals rely on *listening* far more than they rely on talking. The more you listen, the more people telegraph their vulnerabilities, priorities, and fears. The less you reveal about yourself prematurely, the more you keep others guessing. Remember that the *goal of reading the room* is to gather intel that informs your decisions. If you're the one doing all the talking, you lose that crucial advantage.

Creating an Aura of Accessibility—or Mystery

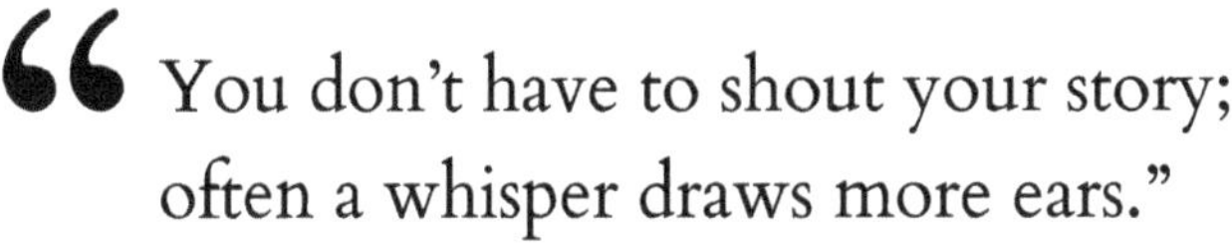

> "You don't have to shout your story; often a whisper draws more ears."

Once you've gathered insights through micro-expressions, body language, and behavioral patterns, you face a critical choice: *How much of yourself do you reveal to the room?* Criminals excel at shaping perceptions. A con artist might adopt an overly friendly persona to lower suspicions, or they might cultivate an air of distant authority to discourage questions.

In legitimate settings, striking the right balance between approachability and mystique can significantly enhance your influence. If you want to foster collaboration, present yourself as open and understanding. Use friendly gestures, nod in agreement, and share small personal anecdotes to build rapport. If you aim to project competence and control in a high-pressure environment, offer concise, confident statements and let others perceive you as somewhat enigmatic. *Your choice should align with the dynamics you have observed.*

> "Strategy without conscience is a blade without a handle—deadly to both its wielder and its target."

Reading a room can be exhilarating, especially once you realize how much more you see compared to the average person. *Yet caution is paramount.* The line between ethically leveraging this skill and descending into manipulation can be alarmingly thin. Criminals cross that line continually because their objectives override moral considerations. They seek personal gain at almost any cost.

In contrast, acting like a lawyer means tempering your heightened awareness with *a sense of justice and accountability.* Recognize that while you might be able to steer a conversation or negotiation in your favor by pushing emotional hot buttons, doing so unscrupulously can erode trust and damage relationships. The point of developing these observations isn't to *control* others by toying with their vulnerabilities but to *anticipate* situations effectively, paving the way for fairer, more balanced outcomes.

Remember, success achieved by manipulation alone is fragile. The moment your methods come to light, you stand to lose respect, credibility, and potential alliances. Truly sustainable success arises from using your heightened perception to find win-win solutions rather than exploiting every weakness you discover. The best lawyers remain formidable precisely because they combine *razor-sharp insight* with ethical practice, ensuring their victories endure scrutiny and foster long-term respect.

The Power of Focus

> You see only what your attention allows—expand that boundary, and a new world emerges."

Try this simple but revealing exercise the next time you are in a group setting. Pick a public place—perhaps a café, a networking event, or even a family gathering. Arrive a few minutes early and *resist the urge to check your phone or engage in small talk.* Instead, observe. Watch how people enter, how they move, and where they gravitate. Note who seems confident, who appears anxious, who tries to command attention, and who slinks into the background.

Pay special attention to micro-expressions. Listen for changes in vocal tone when certain topics emerge. Look at how body language shifts depending on who is speaking and what is being said. This practice can feel like stepping into another dimension, one hidden just beneath the surface of ordinary conversation.

Then, once you've spent a good chunk of time silently cataloging these cues, *pick one person* you've been watching and engage them briefly in conversation. Observe how your prior insights guide your interaction. If you've noticed they are uncomfortable talking about certain subjects, steer clear of those areas or approach them with subtlety. If you sense they enjoy a particular theme—sports, travel, music—lead with that.

In many cases, you'll be astonished at how smoothly and beneficially the interaction flows when you tailor your approach based on nuanced observation. Where others might stumble by blindly guessing what resonates, you'll glide in with an informed strategy. Through this exercise, you begin to understand how criminals slip under the radar while lawyers frame winning arguments: *they see what others don't.*

Turning Observations into Strategic Action

> Observation is only step one—step two is knowing how to capitalize on what you see."

In the chapters ahead, we'll delve deeper into how criminals leverage their observational prowess to execute high-stakes plans, and how lawyers convert similar observational skills into airtight arguments and defenses. For now, the essential lesson is that *the room itself can be a treasure map*, and every small detail—every glance, posture, tone—points you toward hidden markers.

Criminals read the room to identify risks or prime targets; ethical strategists read it to form alliances, solve problems, and position themselves advantageously without burning bridges. Both rely on the same fundamental skill: heightened situational awareness. The difference lies in *what you do* once you've gathered these insights. Do you sow chaos, or do you unify? Do you build honest credibility, or do you capitalize on ignorance and fear?

> A criminal sees opportunity in a room; a lawyer sees obligations as well—but both see the room more clearly than the untrained."

As you refine your ability to read the room, you'll quickly realize that most people remain oblivious to the cues they broadcast. You'll catch the micro-expressions that betray hidden motives, spot the subtle hierarchies at play in a work meeting, and detect the tension that underpins family gatherings long before anyone else acknowledges it. *That heightened awareness is a form of power.* But remember: with power comes responsibility.

In the next chapter, we will explore how criminals and risk-takers evaluate the consequences of their actions—sometimes ignoring them, sometimes using them as leverage. We will dissect the psychology of *calculated risks*, examining why fear paralyzes most individuals while criminals and top lawyers alike seem to dance on the razor's edge with surprising ease. Understanding how to weigh risks intelligently—and how to prepare for potential fallout—will be the next step in your journey toward blending the cunning of a criminal with the protective armor of a lawyer.

For now, let your awareness bloom in every room you enter. Practice scanning the environment before you speak, observe before you commit, and *listen* before you advocate. You'll soon find that many of life's so-called complexities unravel beneath the probing gaze of a well-trained mind. And when the moment comes for you to act, you will do so not as a prey stumbling in the dark, but as a predator—or a protector—who knows exactly how to shape the room, and the conversation, to your advantage.

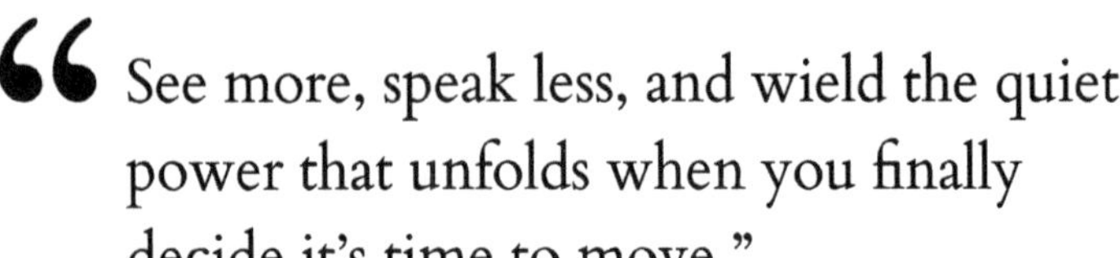

> "See more, speak less, and wield the quiet power that unfolds when you finally decide it's time to move."

4

Calculated Risks

"Those who hesitate remain behind; those who charge in blindly end up lost. True mastery lies in calculated audacity."

The van careened through the nearly deserted streets at three in the morning, its headlights cutting a hard line through the darkness. Inside the vehicle, tension hung as thick as smoke, silent but palpable. Four figures sat with gloved hands and taut nerves, mentally reviewing the final steps of a plan that had dominated their thoughts for months. The heist had seemed flawless on paper: a small private bank with minimal security cameras, a gap in the guard's patrol schedule, and an unmarked back entrance that doubled as a loading zone. Each member of the crew had memorized their role with military precision—like chess pieces, each movement synchronized, each second accounted for. Yet beneath this veneer of confidence lay the unspoken truth that any single oversight could unravel everything.

As the van approached the bank's rear alley, the driver killed the lights. From the outside, it looked like just another dark vehicle momentarily idling under a flickering streetlamp. In that pregnant hush before action, each team member felt the primal rush of fear. The leader swallowed hard, forcing calmness into his posture. *Was the risk truly worth the reward?* It was too late to turn back now, but the question lurked at the edge of every breath. They pressed on, hearts pounding, guided by the careful calculus of risk they had painstakingly crafted—one that would either catapult them into a life of wealth or plunge them into a pit of legal peril.

Calculated Risks—the phrase itself sits at the heart of every audacious move, whether it's a brazen robbery or a groundbreaking entrepreneurial leap. Criminals live by this credo: any operation worth pursuing must balance potential gains against the lurking specter of failure. No one, not even the most seasoned con artist or the most celebrated thief, acts without some modicum of planning. Beneath their daring exteriors, criminals often exhibit a near-obsessive dedication to probability. They scout locations, note the patterns of security guards, gauge how alarm systems interact with local police response times, and anticipate how the slightest detail might cause the entire scheme to collapse.

Of course, criminals neither hold a monopoly on risk-taking nor perfected the art of it in isolation. High-stakes entrepreneurs, visionary artists, and even philanthropic revolutionaries share similar mindsets, though applied in ways that typically respect the boundaries of law. They, too, must face down their fears, weigh potential outcomes, and decide if an uncertain reward justifies the hazards that loom in the shadows. The difference is how they handle the consequences, and that's where the twin lessons of *criminal cunning* and *legal discipline* come into play. By studying how criminals venture into the unknown, we glean vital tactics for navigating ambiguity. By binding those tactics with a keen sense of legality and ethics, we guard against self-destruction.

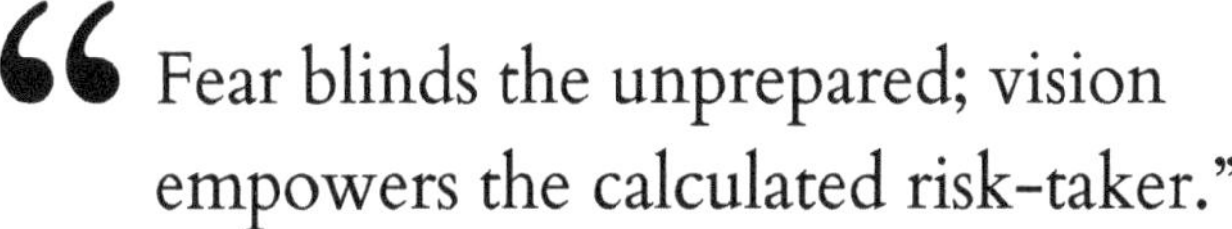

In this chapter, we will dissect the psychology behind bold endeavors, illustrating how the finest criminals and the most effective lawyers manage fear, plan contingencies, and transform what others see as chaos into a controllable playing field. We will also confront a sobering truth: not every risk pays off, and the aftermath of a failed gamble can be devastating. That is why we will explore *a heist gone wrong*, drawing from it the lessons of *too little planning* or *overconfidence*, and how such pitfalls can trip up even the most cunning minds. Ultimately, you will see that the key to successful risk-taking lies not in eradicating fear, but in harnessing it—mastering the delicate balance between cautious restraint and daring action.

Fear, Temptation and Boldness

Before we examine the specific cases and strategies, we must understand the *anatomy of risk*. It starts with *fear*—a fundamental human emotion that keeps us from lunging heedlessly into danger. Fear is a defense mechanism, a primal whisper in the back of our minds urging caution. Criminals are not devoid of fear; on the contrary, they are *intimate* with it. They learn to dance with fear, to let it heighten their senses rather than paralyze them.

Next comes *temptation*, the lure that draws us across the threshold of the unknown. Temptation can take many forms: the glitter of unimaginable wealth, the thrill of outsmarting an opponent, the possibility of fame and acclaim. For a burglar, it might be the prospect of a multimillion-dollar haul. For a budding entrepreneur, it might be disrupting an entire industry. Temptation fans the flames of ambition, pitting fear against the promise of reward.

Finally, *boldness* emerges as the deciding factor: the moment of truth when a person chooses whether to step forward or hold back. Criminals who excel do so because they cultivate a mindset that not only acknowledges the possibility of failure but works tirelessly to mitigate it. They strategize, prepare, and keep fallback plans at the ready. Conversely, those who let excitement override rationality often crash spectacularly.

A skilled lawyer or negotiator mirrors this process in a courtroom or boardroom. Fear of losing a pivotal case might loom large, but so does the temptation of victory, prestige, and hefty legal fees. Boldness manifests as the willingness to adopt an innovative legal argument or to present evidence in a risky but compelling manner. When done right, the reward can be colossal: an acquittal for a client on the brink of conviction or a precedent-setting verdict that cements the lawyer's reputation. When done poorly, it can torpedo a career.

The Art of the Overconfidence Trap

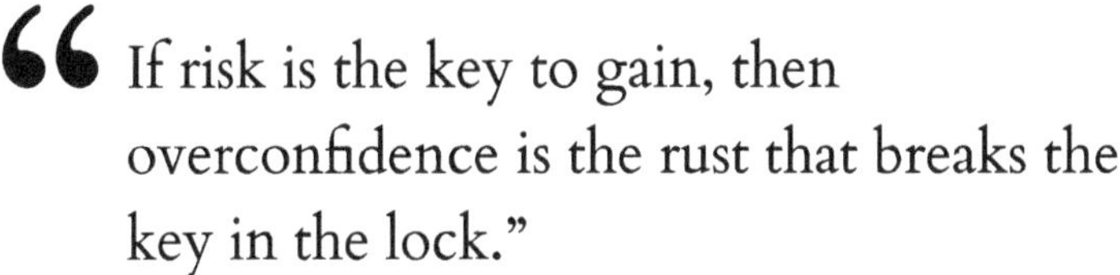

Consider a well-known case from the early 2000s: a team of burglars targeted a midsized jewelry store rumored to hold a rare, priceless necklace. The thieves spent weeks staking out the store's location, memorizing staff schedules, and even running practice drills in a rented warehouse mock-up of the store layout. By all accounts, it was a masterclass in preparation. On the night of the planned heist, they entered through a skylight, bypassed the alarm sensors, and reached the vault without a hitch.

But in the throes of excitement, *they made a fatal assumption*: they believed no one would return to the store after hours, especially given that it was tucked in a quiet suburban neighborhood. Their risk analysis had become muddled by *overconfidence*. As fate would have it, the store owner—an older gentleman known for insomnia—decided to drop by unexpectedly to double-check new inventory deliveries. Spotting a suspicious glare of light inside, he called the police. Although the burglars tried to escape, local patrols had them cornered within minutes. The ringleader, who had never been caught in over a decade of illicit endeavors, found himself face-down on the pavement, handcuffed, and facing a lengthy prison sentence.

The lesson? Even impeccable planning can collapse if *hubris* takes root. This is not just a criminal cautionary tale; overconfidence haunts startups that ignore market research, attorneys who underestimate opposing counsel, and even athletes who assume a weaker opponent poses no threat. Whenever you reach a point where you believe you are unbeatable, you have already opened the first door to failure.

The Criminal's Check-and-Balance

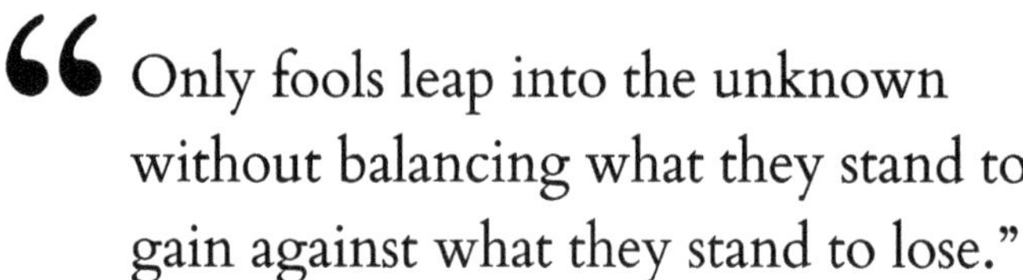

> "Only fools leap into the unknown without balancing what they stand to gain against what they stand to lose."

Criminals employ a mental system of checks and balances that often remains hidden to the casual observer. A seasoned pickpocket might target victims in crowded tourist areas not randomly, but based on the potential payoff (tourists often carry large sums of cash) versus the risk of running into heightened police patrols. A white-collar fraudster might analyze a corporation's internal structure, concluding that the lax auditing standards create enough of a window for them to siphon funds without alerting top executives. In each scenario, the risk-taker tries to determine whether the potential gain justifies the exposure to danger.

Look closely at how con artists gauge their targets. They rarely approach the confident, well-informed individual who asks too many questions; instead, they seek the person who appears isolated, curious, or flattered by attention. They understand that the risk of being caught *increases exponentially* if the mark grows suspicious or involves a third party. By targeting a single, unsuspecting individual, the con artist reduces the risk while maximizing the potential reward.

In a legal or business context, you see a similar dynamic unfold. A lawyer takes on a controversial case not to sabotage their career, but because they see a potentially lucrative settlement or the chance to set a groundbreaking precedent. Likewise, a business executive might pivot into a risky new market because the competitive advantage, if seized early, could dwarf the costs of initial setbacks. Understanding this ratio—*what you gain versus what you might lose*—is crucial for anyone on the precipice of a major decision.

The difference between criminals and legitimate strategists lies in *mitigation and ethics.* Criminals rely on stealth, deception, or intimidation to manage their risks. Ethical strategists rely on carefully crafted contracts, transparent negotiations, or legal frameworks that minimize fallout if a venture stalls. Both sets of individuals, however, share a common trait: they do not blunder in blindly. They *calculate.*

Why Fear Paralyzes the Untrained

> "Paralysis by fear is often just a failure of imagination—when you cannot envision possible success, every risk seems too daunting."

People who have never trained themselves to handle risk are prone to one of two extremes. Either they freeze at the slightest sign of danger or they leap in without any plan at all, driven purely by reckless optimism. The reason for both behaviors is surprisingly similar: *a lack of structured thinking about potential outcomes.*

Fear, when left unmanaged, becomes a magnifying glass that distorts every threat until it appears insurmountable. Your mind fixates on the worst-case scenario, ignoring facts and probabilities. Criminals and lawyers alike combat this by conducting what amounts to a mental "worst-case scenario exercise." Before stepping into a risky venture, they ask themselves: *If it all goes wrong, how do I limit the damage?* For criminals, this might entail planning escape routes or forging fake identities. For lawyers, it might involve drafting contingency clauses in contracts or preparing fallback arguments.

On the flip side, some individuals charge ahead blindly because they *refuse* to entertain the worst-case scenario at all. They rely on luck or charisma, hoping everything will fall into place if they just stay positive. While optimism has its merits, ignoring the inherent dangers of a situation often leads to catastrophic outcomes. Imagine a novice gambler who keeps doubling down on a losing hand, convinced that the "big win" is just around the corner. This is not courage; it's denial. True *calculated risk* arises from facing fear head-on and designing a plan robust enough to navigate unexpected storms.

A Lesson in Preparation and Risk

> "Failing to plan is planning to fail—but over-planning can be just as deadly."

We now circle back to the opening scenario of this chapter, where four thieves embarked on what they believed to be the perfect bank heist. Every detail had been rehearsed, from disabling the alarm system to monitoring the guard's nighttime walk around the premises. In a twist reminiscent of the jewelry store fiasco, fate intervened in a way they had not anticipated. A roving neighborhood patrol, newly assigned to the district, happened to do a drive-by exactly as they breached the back entrance. Their previously mapped-out patrol schedules were now obsolete because of recent staffing changes at the local precinct—changes the thieves had not caught wind of.

In the frantic minutes that followed, the thieves scrambled to adapt their plan. But their strict reliance on outdated data left them cornered. Unlike a professional con artist who might have installed a Plan B—or even Plan C—to handle such an anomaly, these burglars had placed all their chips on the presumed immutability of one set of facts. The result was chaos, panic, and eventual capture. The ringleader later confessed that they had become so convinced of the plan's perfection that they never conceived a viable escape route if new variables arose.

The moral of this story applies as much to legitimate challenges as it does to crime: **circumstances change.** Markets shift, opponents adapt, and new regulations emerge. If your risk analysis relies on *stagnant information* or fails to include alternative outcomes, you set yourself up for disaster. A calculated risk-taker remains dynamic, revisiting assumptions and pivoting strategies at the slightest hint of change.

> A flexible plan bends where a rigid plan breaks—adaptability is the unsung hero of every calculated risk."

The ability to pivot mid-operation is what separates the cunning from the reckless. Criminals who survive multiple heists or cons do so because they continually update their mental maps of the environment, scanning for unforeseen complications. In the same way, a lawyer who excels in court is ever alert to shifts in the judge's demeanor, the jury's reactions, or new evidence introduced by opposing counsel. If something upends their original argument, they adapt swiftly.

Flexible risk strategies rest on one foundational principle: *anticipate change before it arrives.* That might mean regularly checking for new law enforcement policies if you're a criminal, or keeping a close watch on legislative updates if you're a lawyer working a major case. It also means cultivating relationships or networks that keep you informed—something criminals often excel at, forging alliances in the underworld, and something top lawyers do with professional peers who can provide timely tips or legal analyses.

Yet, no matter how prepared you are, the unpredictable can still happen. When it does, the difference between ruin and resilience hinges on whether you have the mental agility—and the humility—to acknowledge that you must pivot. Overconfidence whispers that you can force a square peg into a round hole, but calculated risk invites you to accept reality and *reshape your approach.*

Analyzing Your Own Risk Threshold

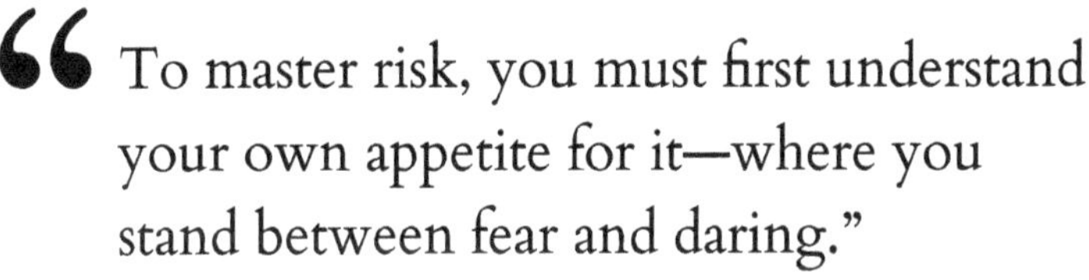

> “To master risk, you must first understand your own appetite for it—where you stand between fear and daring.”

Take a moment to reflect on a significant decision looming in your life. It could be changing jobs, launching a new business, investing your savings in the stock market, or even proposing a bold idea to a skeptical board of directors. Write down all the risks you can perceive, from the most obvious to the hidden, intangible ones that nag at you in the quiet of night. Next, sketch out the possible rewards—financial, emotional, or reputational.

Now, *ask yourself*: Have I truly evaluated the worst-case scenario, or am I avoiding it out of dread? If the worst case occurs, how catastrophic would it be, and do

I have a fallback plan? Conversely, if success materializes, how significant is the reward? By laying this out in black and white, you force your mind to step away from raw anxiety or blind hope, moving instead toward structured, logical thinking.

This exercise mirrors how criminals perform reconnaissance on a target and how lawyers build multiple lines of argument. It is not about guaranteeing success, for no plan can fully shield you from chance. Rather, it's about ensuring you understand the terrain before you venture into it. When you align your level of risk with your readiness to handle setbacks, you set the stage for truly *calculated* risk-taking—a hallmark of both the clever criminal and the strategic legal mind.

Risk as a Shared Language

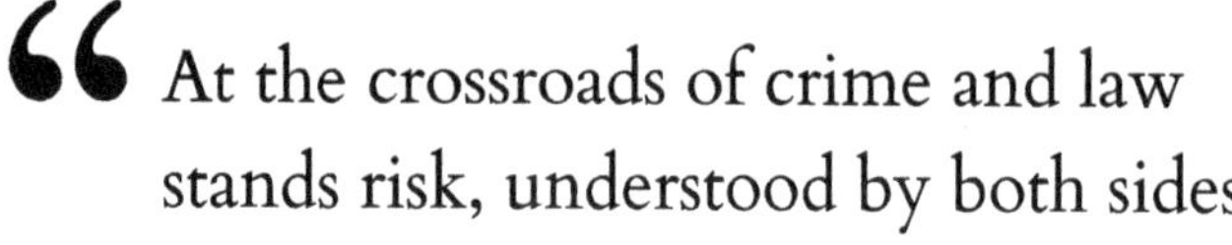

> "At the crossroads of crime and law stands risk, understood by both sides but wielded differently."

Criminals flirt with illegalities, often thriving in the murky overlaps between what is allowed and what is not. Lawyers operate within those same ambiguities, employing them for legal advantage. Both groups comprehend that stepping over the line—be it moral, legal, or simply prudent—can bring downfall. The result is a shared language of *risk management* that transcends moral labels, unifying those who live in the shadows and those who stand in the spotlight.

The cunning criminal sees an open window and thinks, *If I leap, can I land safely with the prize?* The lawyer sees a precarious legal argument and wonders, *If I advance this claim, can I circumvent counterarguments and secure the verdict?* Both weigh variables, assess the cost of failure, and proceed only when they believe the odds favor them. The strategies diverge primarily in execution and in moral or legal accountability.

For you, straddling these perspectives without breaking the law means internalizing the criminals' heightened awareness of risk and pairing it with the lawyer's structured caution and fallback plans. Every major decision becomes a chess match, each move premeditated. You neither cower into inaction nor race forward heedlessly; instead, you move decisively, guided by thorough analysis.

Where to Draw the Line

> Power that dishonors its own conscience is destined for an implosion, swift or slow—but inevitable."

While criminals and lawyers share parallels in how they evaluate risk, the moral boundaries they cross—or refuse to cross—draw a critical dividing line. A con artist might decide that manipulating a lonely individual's emotions is acceptable collateral damage for the sake of a big payday. An ethical negotiator, however, might seek to persuade without deception, aiming to leave all parties feeling their dignity intact.

This moral tension should guide your understanding of *calculated risks*. Even if a particular action promises large returns, is it worth compromising your personal values or permanent reputation? Will success taste as sweet if it burns bridges or sows seeds of distrust? Part of *acting like a lawyer* means foreseeing the long-term ramifications, both legally and ethically. The law, after all, doesn't merely punish the unwise; it can also echo the moral sentiments of society at large, bringing scorn upon those who exploit trust for selfish gain.

By keeping ethics in focus, you harness the strongest elements of both mindsets. You adopt the criminal's fearless pursuit of advantage—tempered by the lawyer's commitment to sustainability, legality, and moral clarity. That is how you ascend to positions of genuine power rather than fleeting influence.

Embracing and Mastering Uncertainty

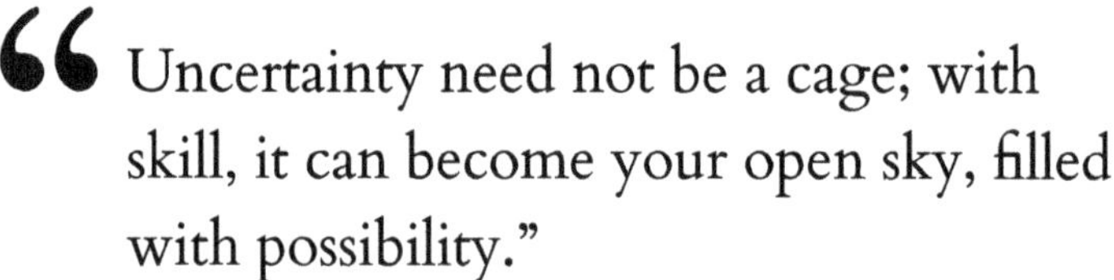

> "Uncertainty need not be a cage; with skill, it can become your open sky, filled with possibility."

Calculated risks will always involve uncertainty. That is the very nature of gambling on an unknown future. But uncertain does not have to mean reckless or ill-prepared. The greatest strategists—on either side of the law—excel precisely because they have made an ally of uncertainty. They treat it as a terrain to be mapped, not a monster to be fled.

As this chapter draws to a close, remember that your capacity for calculated risk is a muscle. It grows stronger every time you analyze a situation thoroughly and navigate the tension between fear and temptation. It matures every time you adapt to the unexpected, remain flexible in the face of shifting circumstances, and maintain an unwavering sense of ethics.

We have glimpsed the pitfalls of overconfidence, the crippling power of unmanaged fear, and the brilliance of those who plan for success by imagining failure. In criminal circles, these lessons surface in the cunning of a well-orchestrated con and the meltdown of a sloppy burglary. In legal spheres, they shine in the masterful argument that secures a client's freedom and the disastrous oversight that leads to professional disgrace.

You are now ready to weave these lessons into the broader tapestry of the *Criminal Mindset*—to think with a criminal's audacity while operating under the protective counsel of legal wisdom. In our next step, we will pivot to **Part II: Legal Armor**, where we explore how mastery of the law can serve as both shield and sword. You will see how the cunning gleaned from criminals becomes exponentially more powerful when reinforced by legal knowledge that keeps you secure from the repercussions of a careless gamble.

For the moment, let your mind settle on the essential truth behind this chapter: *great leaps forward often carry equal parts peril and promise*. The brilliance of a plan is measured not merely by the reward it can bring, but by how well it contends with the realities of setback and adversity. Embrace your fears, weigh them against your goals, and then step forward with the poise and confidence that only thorough preparation can grant. In that quiet space between caution and courage, you will discover a realm of opportunities invisible to the timid and unattainable to the reckless.

> Risk and reward are two sides of the same coin—lift it, turn it, examine its edges. Only then can you decide whether it's worth the toss."

PART II

Legal Armor

5
The Law as a Weapon

> "The best criminal isn't the one who avoids getting caught—it's the one who knows how to stay within the gray areas of legality."

A subdued hush settled over the courthouse corridors as the midday lull set in. Most judges and clerks were either at lunch or catching a brief moment of respite between hearings. The overhead lights cast an even, almost clinical glow upon the linoleum floors. Amid this quiet, a single figure strode purposefully down the hallway. He was dressed in a crisp, tailored black suit and carried a slim leather briefcase that he set down momentarily outside Courtroom 7. With deliberate poise, he straightened his tie, ran a hand over his immaculate hair, and pushed open the heavy wooden door.

Inside the courtroom, a few curious eyes turned his way: reporters scribbling notes for a mid-profile trial, the weary court stenographer adjusting her equipment, and a bailiff who sized him up more out of routine than suspicion. No one realized that the figure, a man who looked every inch the typical defense attorney, was in fact a key player in a carefully orchestrated scheme. While he possessed all the credentials of a legitimate advocate—passed the bar, had his name on a magnificently built chambers—his real mastery lay in manipulating the very laws he was sworn to uphold.

If you observed closely, you might have noticed a subtle gleam in his gaze, as though he were about to engage in a strategic game of chess. For months, he had studied every line of the penal code relevant to his client's case, not simply to defend against accusations, but to exploit subtle loopholes buried in precedential rulings and ambiguous legal language. By the time he reached his seat, he had no doubt that he could steer the trial's outcome in his favor. This was a man who understood that *the law is not always a fortress of justice—it can be a weapon, wielded skillfully by those who grasp its intricacies.*

That scene, while fictionalized, cuts to the core of our focus in this chapter: *the law as a weapon.* Contrary to how many people view it, the law is not just a set of rigid rules that either convict or absolve. Rather, in the hands of a cunning operator—whether that be a white-collar criminal or an accomplished advocate—the law can serve as both shield and sword. Criminals often dance at the edges of legality, seeking the gray areas where moral and statutory lines blur. Lawyers, for their part, find ways to stretch or contract these lines, shaping narratives to their client's advantage. In these overlapping zones of ambiguity, *true power* emerges, uniting the boldness of a criminal's mindset with the precision of legal discipline.

Seeing the Law as More Than Boundaries

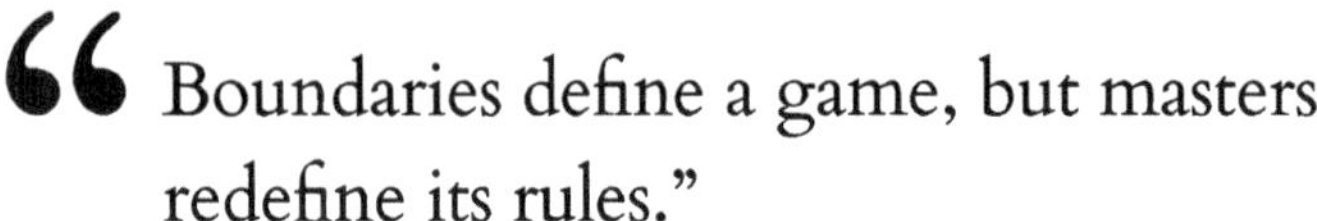

> Boundaries define a game, but masters redefine its rules."

Most people approach the law with a measure of trepidation, seeing it as a barrier that confines their actions within a set of permissible standards. They abide by it largely out of fear of punishment. Criminals, however, view the law differently. They see it as a puzzle to be solved, a living code that can be analyzed for vulnerabilities. Their question is not, "What can I do to avoid breaking the law?" but rather, "How can I use the wording, structure, and enforcement mechanisms of this law to further my aims?" That might mean exploiting bureaucratic red tape, forging documents that mimic the style and language of legal forms, or capitalizing on slow-moving regulatory bodies that rarely communicate with each other.

Attorneys, conversely, are taught to interpret and apply the law in a manner that benefits their clients. Yet the most effective lawyers are not simply reciting statutes; they're *constantly testing the edges of legal interpretation.*

They note how precedent has shifted over the years, how cultural sentiment can impact a judge's ruling, or how legislative changes might open a back door to a compelling defense. This perspective of *law as malleable* rather than *absolute* is what distinguishes an average attorney from a virtuoso.

Criminals might operate outside or at the fringes of the law, but a well-versed attorney operates fully within it—yet still harnesses the flexibility that exists between its lines. When you learn to see the law in this layered way, you arm yourself with a powerful tool: *you no longer fear legal codes as immovable constraints, but recognize them as frameworks that can be navigated.*

The Gray Areas—Where Law and Cunning Collide

> Society assumes 'black or white,' but power resides in the subtle shades of gray."

In nearly every legal system, no matter how comprehensive, there are gray areas—zones of ambiguity that arise when statutes are poorly worded, outdated, or riddled with exceptions. These loopholes are the gateways that resourceful criminals use to avoid prosecution. They are also the footholds that clever lawyers rely on to dismantle seemingly ironclad cases.

Consider a real-world parallel: multinational corporations sometimes choose to incorporate in jurisdictions with lenient tax laws or complicated legal structures. These companies aren't outright breaking any statutes; they're simply leveraging the fact that international tax codes do not align perfectly, creating opportunities to shift money across borders with minimal oversight. Are they criminals? Legally, no—not if everything remains on paper and they file all required documents, albeit in a labyrinthine manner that keeps regulators guessing. Morally, opinions might vary. *But the point remains:* they are using the law's gaps and inconsistencies to their advantage.

A well-trained attorney, especially one who represents such corporations, knows exactly how to "translate" these gaps into a legitimate legal strategy. In many ways, they mirror the cunning of a criminal. They scour the law for precedents that support their client's position and highlight ambiguities that cast doubt on the opposing side's arguments. Their aim is not deception but *interpretation.* They are not forging or faking documents; they are, however, shaping the narrative so the law bends in their favor.

Documents, Contracts and Technicalities

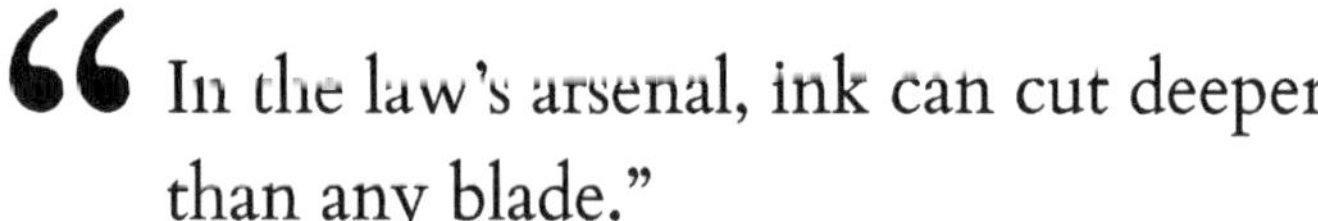

Criminals and lawyers alike understand the importance of paper—a contract, a license, a court filing. It's often said that the pen is mightier than the sword, and nowhere is this more evident than in the courtroom. The existence of a single signed document can dramatically alter the course of a dispute.

Criminals might forge wills, alter deeds, or create fictitious companies on paper, aiming to disguise the flow of money or property. Lawyers, on the other hand, draft contracts with enough fine print to fill a library, each clause carefully worded to protect their client from future litigation. A skilled advocate knows that the best offense might be hidden in paragraph 28, subsection C of an agreement that no layperson ever fully reads.

Where criminals might rely on doctored signatures, attorneys depend on the strategic structuring of clauses to ensure that if a conflict arises, their client is either blameless or at least armed with a strong defense. In many ways, it's two sides of the same coin: *the manipulation of language to create a legal advantage.* One side wades into illegal territory by forging documents, while the other remains legitimate by meticulously verifying every signature, stamp, and notary. Yet both practices hinge on the same foundational truth: *most people do not question what's written on paper unless compelled to do so.*

Loopholes and Technicalities

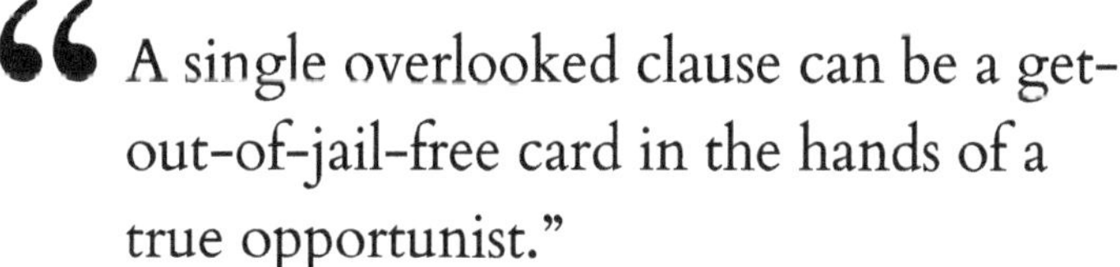

“A single overlooked clause can be a get-out-of-jail-free card in the hands of a true opportunist.”

Take, for instance, a con artist who orchestrates an elaborate pyramid scheme. They might structure their business in such a way that they never overtly promise guaranteed returns. Instead, they use language that implies success without explicitly stating it. If regulators investigate, the con artist can point to carefully worded disclaimers, maintaining they never claimed *certainty*. Is it ethical? Absolutely not. Is it illegal? That depends on how the courts interpret the disclaimers.

That shadowy approach mirrors what a savvy corporate lawyer might do in a complex merger agreement—insert carefully calibrated language that neither breaks the law nor outright deceives but leaves enough wiggle room for future legal maneuvering. If the opposing party fails to read the fine print or interpret the contract with the same level of diligence, they might find themselves at a severe disadvantage when issues arise.

This notion—that subtle wording can tip the balance—reinforces how criminals and lawyers both exploit the maze of language. Each section, each clause, each phrase, can act like a hidden tripwire, waiting for the right moment to be triggered in court. The difference, naturally, is in the ultimate goals and methods. While the criminal thrives on subterfuge, the ethical lawyer works within the law, ensuring that any "trap" they set adheres to procedural fairness and established rules of interpretation. Yet the *mechanics of cunning* remain strikingly similar.

Ethical Versus Unethical—Where Does the Line Lie?

A weapon in noble hands is a shield for the weak; in selfish hands, it brings havoc."

The tension between criminal exploitation of legal gaps and a lawyer's advocacy for clients raises a profound question: *Where does the line lie between strategic brilliance and unethical conduct?* A defense lawyer who discredits a witness using minor inconsistencies might be employing a fair tactic or might be skirting the edges of integrity if they knowingly twist a witness's words.

Lawyers are bound by professional codes of conduct. These standards uphold honesty before the court and a duty to provide zealous representation without resorting to outright deception. Criminals, conversely, are not bound by such rules. Their single-minded focus on personal gain eclipses moral or ethical considerations. Yet the methods each group employs can appear eerily similar: close examination of records, leveraging language ambiguities, and reframing narratives to fit their desired outcome.

This is why, as you learn to *use the law as a weapon*, you must keep your moral compass intact. Mastering the law's intricacies can bestow tremendous power, but it also poses a temptation to overstep. It is one thing to dismantle a flawed claim or highlight legitimate errors in an opponent's argument; it's another to spin false narratives or bury critical evidence. The latter is what drags a skilled lawyer into the territory of criminal complicity, a place where the lines between counselor and conspirator blur.

Shielding Yourself with Legal Knowledge

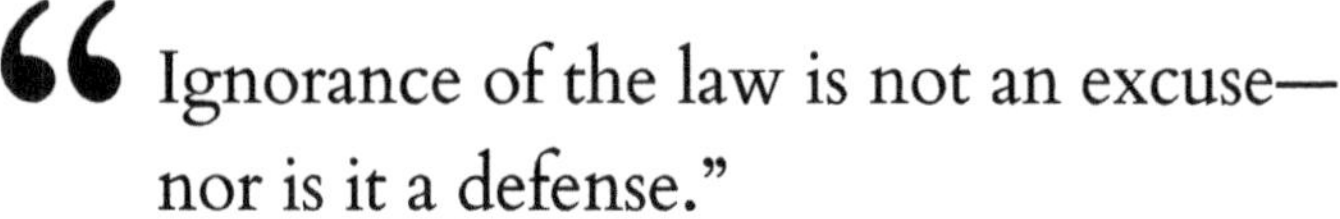

> "Ignorance of the law is not an excuse—nor is it a defense."

One of the fundamental ways to avoid slipping into the wrong side of the ethical divide is to arm yourself with a thorough understanding of legal principles. People often think they should leave law to the "experts," but criminals prove that anyone can glean enough knowledge to navigate legal systems in cunning ways. Why shouldn't the average citizen, aspiring entrepreneur, or ambitious professional do the same—*but for legitimate ends*?

Learning the basics of contract law, corporate governance, or regulatory compliance can shield you from fraudulent partnerships or exploitative contracts. Even a rudimentary grasp of legal procedure can protect you from malicious litigation, ensuring you don't inadvertently incriminate yourself or sign away crucial rights. A cunning criminal invests time to study the system they plan to game; a wise professional should invest equally in understanding the system they plan to use ethically.

This dedication to self-education extends beyond memorizing statutes. It encompasses developing an instinct for *potential pitfalls*—knowing that if a proposal or agreement seems too good to be true, it probably masks hidden clauses or conditions that can bite back later. It also means recognizing your own limitations: if a matter grows too complex, consult an expert who can guide you.

Case in Point: The Ambiguous Contract Clause

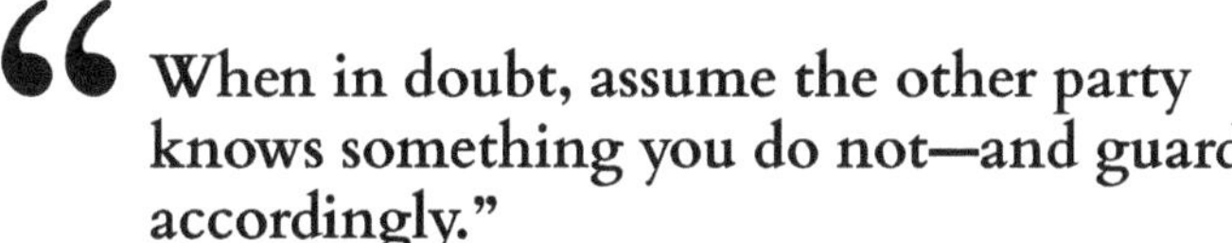

> **"When in doubt, assume the other party knows something you do not—and guard accordingly."**

Imagine a scenario where you're negotiating a lucrative business deal. The contract includes a clause regarding future royalties that might be owed if certain performance metrics are met. The language reads: "Royalties will be disbursed provided the quarterly benchmarks remain sufficiently profitable." At a glance, this might seem harmless. Yet an attorney with a sharp eye would immediately question the term *sufficiently profitable.* What does that mean in numbers? Who determines it, and by what formula?

A criminally minded individual might leave that language intentionally vague, planning to claim that the benchmarks were never met, thus withholding royalties. An honest but inexperienced person might sign the contract, only to discover too late that their definition of "sufficiently profitable" differs drastically from the other party's. A savvy lawyer, aware that an ambiguous term can be manipulated, would insist on clarifying it in numerical terms: "a net profit of at least 10% over the prior quarter," for example.

In real life, entire lawsuits can hinge on such a phrase. This is how the law becomes a battleground, with each side using contract clauses as ammunition in a war of interpretations. The criminal engineer of that vague language wins if they manage to keep everything murky enough to avoid legal accountability, while the unprepared signee suffers the consequences. Conversely, a prepared lawyer disarms that bomb before it's planted, ensuring that neither side can turn it into a hidden landmine.

From Contracts to Courtrooms

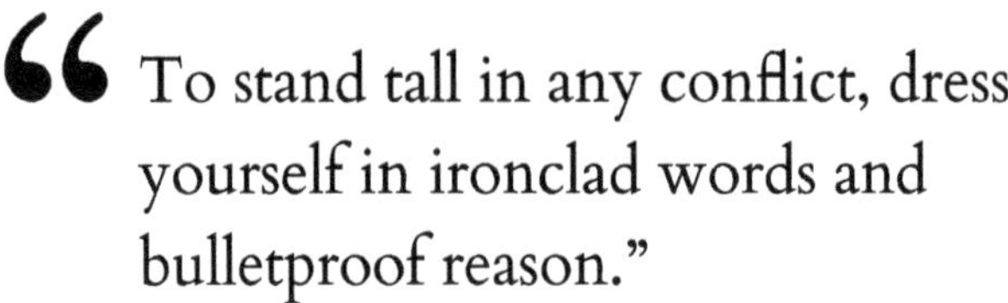

Knowing how criminals exploit legal gaps can empower you to shield yourself or your cause effectively. Just as criminals learn to spot weaknesses in security systems, you can learn to spot loopholes, ambiguous phrasing, and structural flaws in agreements or legal procedures. You do not have to be an attorney to incorporate these protective measures into your life—whether you're launching a small business, signing a property lease, or volunteering for a nonprofit that needs oversight of its funding.

The same strategies that criminals use to conceal their wrongdoing—multiple shell companies, layered contractual obligations, offshore bank accounts—can hint at how you might want to *structure your defenses*. It might mean thorough due diligence on potential partners, using contractual clauses that explicitly outline each party's obligations, or ensuring that your business processes leave an organized paper trail that can withstand scrutiny.

Attorneys, in particular, are adept at constructing these layers of defense. They anticipate challenges to their client's position and frame documents accordingly. Think of it as *proactive lawyering*. A brilliant example is how a corporate attorney might embed arbitration clauses to prevent costly lawsuits, or specify the jurisdiction that favors their client's interests should disputes arise. Criminals do something similar: they orchestrate jurisdictional mazes to confound law enforcement. Both are applying the principle of "preparation beats reaction" by controlling the field of legal play before the opposing side can even mount a challenge.

Harnessing the Power of Legal Language Responsibly

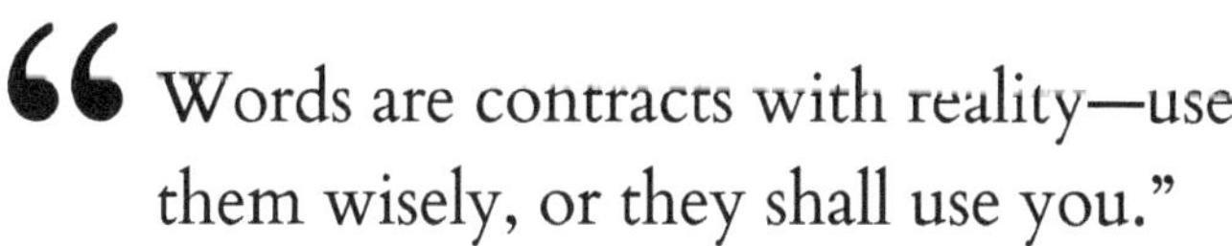

Language is the linchpin that holds all legal structures together. It defines what is a crime, what is a valid contract, and what obligations must be fulfilled. When you craft your words with foresight, you effectively write a mini-constitution that governs the outcome of your dealings. Conversely, a careless phrase can become a ticking time bomb.

This is why criminals invest time in forging documents that appear authentic, and it is why skilled lawyers rewrite, edit, and finalize contracts multiple times before handing them to clients. Every word is a potential bullet, either fired at the opponent or boomeranging back at you. It's a dance of semantics, but with real-world stakes.

Yet the triumph of language lies not in deception but in clarity. The more precise you are, the fewer gaps you leave for adversaries to exploit. Criminals thrive on vague language because it gives them room to maneuver. Ethical practitioners strive for unambiguous wording, aware that clarity is the bedrock of fairness and accountability.

> “Mastery is born at the intersection of practicality, cunning, and moral grounding.”

By this point, you have explored how criminals and lawyers each manipulate or navigate legal frameworks to serve their agendas. You have seen how gray areas, loopholes, and ambiguous language can serve as both cloak and dagger. Now, imagine harnessing that awareness without tipping into the unethical behaviors that characterize the criminal world.

In practical terms, acting like a lawyer means developing an intrinsic respect for the law's protective measures: due process, equal representation, the requirement of evidence. Thinking like a criminal means never overlooking the cracks in the legal foundation—no matter how minor. You remain on high alert for ways to secure an advantage, all while respecting the overarching moral boundaries that keep you rooted in legitimate practice.

This fusion of mindsets creates *a strategic equilibrium*, where you are neither naive about the system's vulnerabilities nor opportunistically violating them. Instead, you become the rare individual who can read a contract or a legal code with the eye of a hawk, spotting any detail that might later pivot the entire outcome of a negotiation, lawsuit, or deal. You become adept at leveraging the law not as a cage but as a structure you can navigate with foresight.

> Those who read the law as a series of walls remain trapped; those who see doors and passageways transcend the ordinary."

As we close this chapter, consider how your own life might change if you perceived the law as a dynamic tool rather than a static set of do's and don'ts. Imagine the advantage you'd have in business ventures, negotiations, and personal affairs. Envision how bulletproof your defenses would be if you learned to spot and seal the cracks criminals exploit.

This is more than an intellectual exercise; it is a recalibration of how you engage with the world. When criminals treat the law as a puzzle, they often succeed because others remain complacent, trusting in superficial compliance. When lawyers stretch the law through novel arguments, they often triumph because opponents underestimate the malleability of statutes. By blending both perspectives, you stand at the forefront of a new type of strategic power—one steeped in cunning and tempered by conscience.

We now move into the next chapters with a firm understanding that the law can be both a sword and a shield, a trap for the unwary and a treasure map for the insightful. *Part II: Legal Armor* is about to unfold in greater depth, providing you with the fundamental building blocks of defense, negotiation, and persuasive advocacy. As you progress, remember that a powerful mind does not shy away from complexity; it embraces the intricate nature of law and recognizes the underlying artistry of shaping outcomes to your advantage.

In forging ahead, never lose sight of the quote that anchors this chapter: ***"The best criminal isn't the one who avoids getting caught—it's the one who knows how to stay within the gray areas of legality."*** Let it serve as a reminder that knowledge of the law is not simply about avoiding a guilty verdict; it's about positioning yourself strategically in a world where every word, every contract, every precedent can tilt the scales. If you can stay attuned to the moral lines that define ethical conduct, your power will not only be formidable—it will be sustainable.

The journey continues. The armor awaits. Prepare to wield the law with both mastery and integrity, and in doing so, claim the terrain that few dare to occupy. For the shadows and the spotlight are closer than most realize, and the difference often lies in how deftly you navigate the boundaries that connect them.

6
Negotiating with Power

"Words are the gentlest chains—and when wielded well, they can bind more tightly than steel."

An unrelenting desert sun baked the small border outpost where two figures faced each other across a rickety wooden table. To one side sat a seasoned smuggler with weathered hands and dark, calculating eyes. Opposite him was a young officer of the local militia, fresh in uniform but already drowning in the complexities of patrolling the lawless expanse. Both men wanted something only the other could grant. The officer longed for information about a notorious cartel rumored to be operating nearby. The smuggler, in turn, needed safe passage through the region without harassment or confiscation of his goods. Neither trusted the other, but each recognized that the cost of open hostilities would be steep and likely fruitless.

In a space devoid of gavel or contract, they began to talk. Their conversation twisted and turned like a rattlesnake on scorching sand. Threats hovered in the background, yet the exchange remained polite—tinged with false camaraderie and guarded smiles. Anyone watching from afar might have mistaken it for a casual chat between acquaintances. But in reality, it was a high-stakes *negotiation*, each man angling to secure the biggest slice of advantage without surrendering too much in return. By the time the sun slipped below the horizon, an agreement materialized. The smuggler offered a tip on a rival group's hideout while the officer granted him a three-day window of unobstructed travel.

That raw scene, unfolding far from the polished floors of any courtroom, laid bare the primal heartbeat of negotiation. Beneath the formalities of business deals and legal contracts lies an elemental transaction—*I have something you want; you have something I need; how do we strike a balance?* In this chapter, we explore how the synergy of criminal cunning and legal discipline can transform ordinary conversation into a masterclass in negotiation. Lawyers, who have honed the art of argument, show us how to weave logic and rhetoric into a persuasive tapestry that can sway hearts and minds. Criminals, always on the lookout for leverage, remind us never to discount hidden angles or unspoken vulnerabilities. Together, these perspectives hold the key to negotiating with power, ensuring that you emerge not just with a truce, but with a victory.

From Confrontation to Collaboration

No better weapon exists than a calm mind guided by persuasive words."

Many imagine a courtroom as a battleground, a place of fierce accusations and defiant defenses. Yet the most accomplished attorneys realize that genuine power often stems from *collaboration rather than confrontation.* A skilled lawyer knows how to read an opposing counsel's fears and motivations, then find a middle ground that grants both sides enough satisfaction to sign on the dotted line. This is not a betrayal of one's client; rather, it's a recognition that negotiations thrive on shared interests.

Consider how a criminal might exploit tension, sow discord, and exploit each rift to their advantage. Lawyers, while rarely seeking chaos, can channel a similar insight: *any reveal of tension can be negotiated to one's benefit—if you're the one steering the conversation.* Imagine a real estate dispute where the other party fixates on holding the deed to a property, but you uncover that their true pain point is the cost of renovations. By proposing a solution that addresses those financial woes, you mitigate a potential clash and create a situation where both parties gain.

Criminal cunning surfaces in the lawyer's approach to gleaning hidden pressure points. They ask open-ended questions, watch for flickers of anxiety or excitement, and infer the intangible factors that might be shaping the other party's stance. When it works, the result can be a seamless, almost friendly negotiation that leaves outsiders oblivious to the layers of strategy woven beneath each smile.

Confidence, Not Arrogance

> A swollen ego roars, but true confidence often whispers—and still commands the room."

Negotiations unravel when one side exudes haughty arrogance. Bluffs and bravado might seem effective in the short term, but they risk provoking the other party or leading them to question your credibility. In contrast, both criminals and lawyers who survive—and *thrive*—over the long haul understand the nuanced difference between arrogance and *assured poise.*

A criminal mastermind stepping into a risky arrangement—let's say the trade of stolen goods—projects calm proficiency rather than chest-thumping aggression. He or she knows that too much swagger can unsettle potential partners, stir suspicions, or trigger resentments. Similarly, an attorney stepping into a high-stakes settlement conference recognizes that quiet confidence is disarming, compelling the other side to lean in rather than recoil. The moment you strain to prove superiority, you lose the subtle advantage of controlling the flow.

This underscores the importance of mastering your nonverbal cues. Keep your shoulders squared but relaxed. Let your gaze meet the other party's without flinching or glaring. Show you are listening—*genuinely* listening—by letting a beat of silence pass before you respond. Such a stance invites dialogue and conveys that you're not desperate, but neither are you dismissive of the person you face.

Framing the Deal

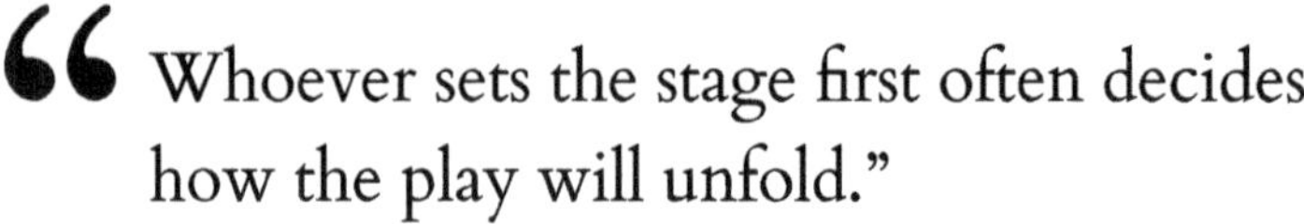

> "Whoever sets the stage first often decides how the play will unfold."

Criminals excel at framing scenarios to their advantage, often by taking charge of how a situation is initially perceived. A pickpocket working a crowd might distract attention with a staged commotion; a con artist might craft a sob story to soften a target's defenses. Attorneys do something similar—though within ethical boundaries—by presenting a carefully curated narrative early in negotiations. If you set the context, the other party must react to *your* framing.

In a legal negotiation, for instance, one might begin by emphasizing the *shared* goals both sides have. If the matter is a contract dispute, a lawyer might open with: "We're all interested in avoiding lengthy litigation and maintaining good business relations, right?" That single statement can tilt the conversation away from a combative showdown toward a more amicable resolution. The question is no longer whether to settle but *how* to settle.

In personal negotiations—be it a salary discussion or a delicate family matter—framing also proves crucial. If you want a pay increase, do you walk into your supervisor's office declaring, "I deserve more money," or do you highlight how "These recent successes have saved the company thousands of dollars, and continuing that momentum is my top priority"? The second approach frames the discussion around shared benefits, not raw demands.

The Mirror Principle

A skilled negotiator becomes a mirror—showing the other side their own desires until they believe you share the same reflection."

Criminals who rely on social engineering use mirroring to appear trustworthy. They reflect their target's body language, speech patterns, and even emotional tone. The target, seeing themselves (or aspects of themselves) in the criminal, lowers their guard. In a more legitimate setting, attorneys employ a similar tactic by acknowledging and validating the opposing side's perspective.

This *doesn't* mean conceding your position. Rather, it's a psychological tactic: when someone feels understood, they unconsciously shift from defending themselves to engaging more openly. A lawyer might say, "I understand why your client feels this contract clause is unfair; if I were in your shoes, I'd have similar concerns." That moment of empathy does not forfeit the lawyer's stance. Instead, it mirrors the opponent's worries so effectively that tensions thaw, and the path to compromise widens.

This principle can revolutionize how you negotiate daily obstacles, from finalizing a car purchase to resolving disputes with neighbors. People generally resist confrontation but gravitate toward empathy. If you reflect their concerns without outright surrendering, you disarm them on a psychological level, making them more receptive to your eventual requests.

Knowing When to Retreat

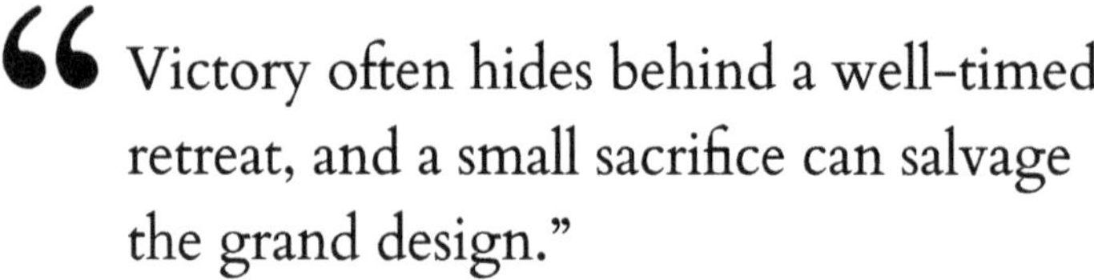

> "Victory often hides behind a well-timed retreat, and a small sacrifice can salvage the grand design."

Criminal cunning thrives on the ability to withdraw tactically. A burglar might abandon one route if an unexpected guard appears, pivoting to another entry without scrapping the entire plan. An illegal arms dealer might agree to forfeit a fraction of profit to placate a suspicious buyer, preserving the larger deal and avoiding a blow-up. Lawyers mirror this mindset when they offer a calculated concession at just the right juncture.

In a negotiation, a concession should never be a sign of weakness. Instead, it should be a tool of exchange. You grant a minor point that matters deeply to the other side but is less critical to your core aims. In doing so, you not only build goodwill, you also gain leverage to demand something in return. A savvy negotiator orchestrates these trade-offs so that by the end, the ledger is in their favor even if a few minor surrenders have been made along the way.

The key is to identify which aspects of your position are truly negotiable. If you concede something that undergirds your entire stance, you risk destabilizing the negotiation altogether. Criminals call it "not giving away the store," while lawyers label it "preserving the essential terms." Both approaches underscore that power is not about refusing to budge; it's about budging in the precise spots that bolster your overall standing.

Turning Up the Heat

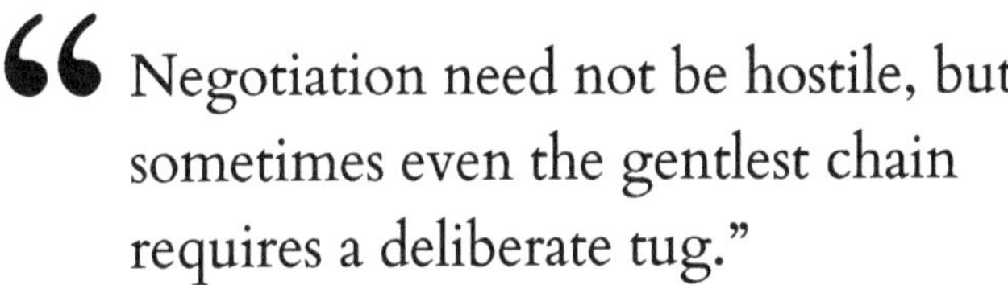

Some negotiations inevitably reach an impasse. Perhaps the other side digs in, believing you can be pushed to yield. Or maybe they interpret your cooperative nature as a sign of vulnerability. In such moments, criminals might subtly invoke a threat—an implied promise of consequence if demands aren't met. Lawyers, on the other hand, have a more refined mechanism: *legal precedent, injunctions, or the looming possibility of court intervention.*

A litigator might remind the opposing counsel, politely yet firmly, of past cases where judges awarded substantial damages in situations strikingly similar to the current one. The implication is clear: concede now or risk a far harsher outcome in court. This method harnesses an external authority—case law, or the notion of a judge's ruling—to impart gravity without degenerating into personal threats.

In everyday negotiations, you can mimic this approach by calmly underscoring potential outcomes if an agreement fails. Perhaps you highlight that a missed deadline will jeopardize a joint project, or that certain promotional opportunities will vanish if the other side remains uncooperative. The aim is not to bully, but to remind the other party that life proceeds with or without their assent, and refusing to find common ground comes with consequences.

The Mock Negotiation—A Brief Scenario

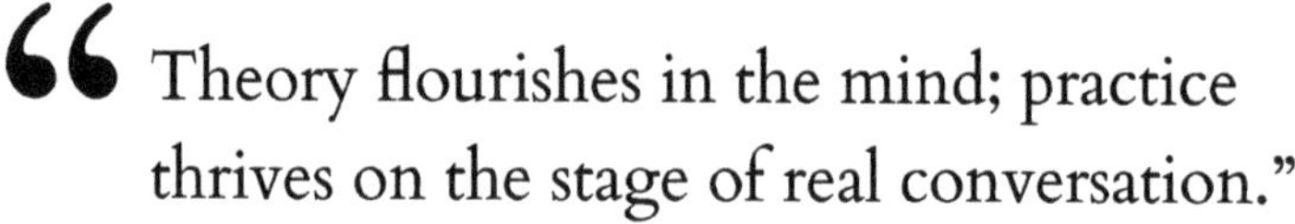

Imagine you're about to negotiate a big salary hike. You've put in more hours than any colleague, secured major clients, and catapulted sales figures. Your manager, swamped with budget constraints, is wary of increasing costs but fears losing top talent. As you step into her office, you sense tension in the air—a fear that you might be about to deliver an ultimatum.

Here's a compact script illustrating how the discussion might unfold in a *criminal-lawmaker fusion style*:

You (poised, calm, and prepared to frame the talk): "I'm grateful for the challenges and responsibilities I've had here. Over the last quarter, our new clients and expanded partnerships have generated a 20% revenue boost. I believe my role in that growth merits a conversation about how I can continue to contribute at my highest level."

You start by emphasizing shared goals and framing the negotiation around collaboration. You mirror your manager's concerns about budget but quickly pivot to highlight how your unique contributions bring tangible value.

Manager (hesitant, arms folded): "We appreciate your work, but the budget is tight. Even though your performance is stellar, we have to consider the overall financial picture."

You read her body language—closed off, leaning away—and respond with empathy:

You (mirroring her concerns, offering a concession): "I realize budgeting is a balancing act. It might help if we structure my compensation in a way that aligns with continued success—something like a base increase plus performance-based bonuses. That way, we both feel comfortable with the investment."

Note the measured concession: you're not demanding an immediate lump sum. You pivot to a performance metric that still ensures your success is rewarded.

Manager (shoulders relaxing): "Okay, performance-based makes sense. Let's talk specifics."

By mirroring her worries about cost and offering a strategic compromise, you transform a potentially confrontational meeting into a constructive dialogue.

You've used a bit of criminal insight (anticipating objections, spotting vulnerabilities) blended with lawyerly structure (framing the conversation around measurable, contractual terms). The result? A feasible agreement that respects both sides' priorities.

Reading the Room—Timing and Tone

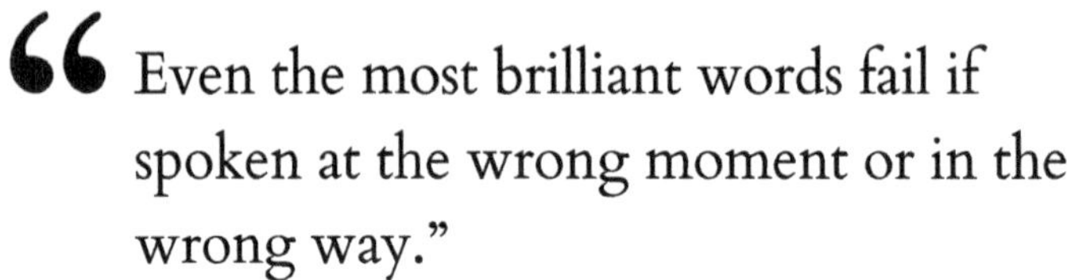

Recall from the earlier chapters how criminals rely on vigilance—the art of reading subtle cues in an environment—and how attorneys adjust arguments based on a judge's mood or a jury's shifting sympathies. In negotiation, reading the room is paramount. If you sense impatience, tighten your points. If you detect openness, elaborate further. If the other party grows defensive, revisit an earlier, friendlier note.

Reading the room also involves sensing when the conversation reaches a natural inflection point—often signaled by a lull or a question that hangs in the air. A skilled negotiator seizes that moment to pivot the discussion in a new direction or to place a carefully timed proposal on the table. The goal is to avoid pushing relentlessly when the other side needs a mental breather, but also not to stall unnecessarily when momentum is on your side.

Exiting with Dignity

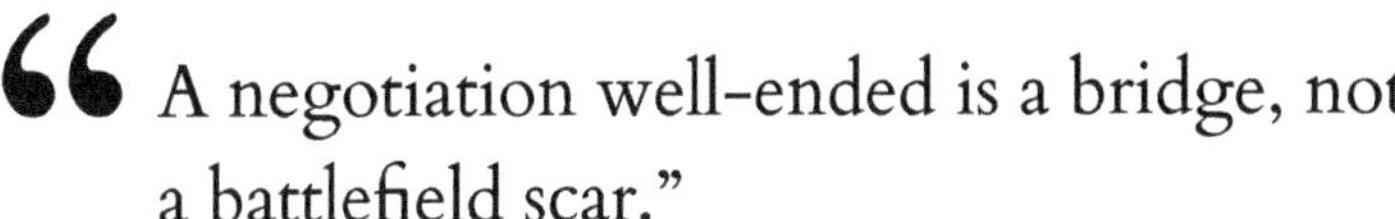

> “A negotiation well-ended is a bridge, not a battlefield scar.”

Even after you’ve secured the terms you desire, the manner in which you close a negotiation can cast long shadows on your future dealings. Criminals, having concluded a successful deal, often withdraw discreetly, leaving minimal resentment or suspicion. Lawyers know that a settlement accompanied by mutual respect can lead to fewer disputes down the line.

In practical terms, this means cementing the agreement in writing—concise, clear, and free from ambiguous language. A handshake and a handshake alone can be interpreted too loosely, a risk criminals accept when operating outside the law but one you don’t want to take if you’re aiming to preserve relationships and credibility. An attorney would advise you to get everything documented: the concessions made, the responsibilities each party assumes, and a straightforward timeline for compliance.

End on a note of goodwill. Thank the other party for their cooperation. This matters even if the negotiation had moments of tension. You’re imprinting a final memory that can influence how they’ll behave in future interactions. People rarely forget how a negotiation makes them *feel*, and if they emerge with bruised pride, they might seek retribution later. If they walk away feeling respected, they're more likely to honor and even reinforce the deal.

Negotiating with Power—The Grand Synthesis

> Persuasion flows from understanding both the cracks and the pillars in another's fortress of belief."

The art of negotiation, at its highest level, draws from the precise discipline of a lawyer and the cunning adaptability of a criminal. Lawyers remind us that words matter, that a well-structured argument can achieve more than any brute force. Criminals illustrate how leverage, timing, and a keen sense of the other party's weaknesses can tip the scales in your favor. By blending both perspectives, you learn to approach negotiations as a tapestry of subtle moves rather than a blunt exchange of demands.

Through it all, ethics remain your anchor. While criminals might blur moral lines to win, your goal is to use these skills within a framework of integrity. Lying, bullying, or deceiving might bring short-term gains, but they invariably seed long-term consequences. True power emerges when you harness strategic insight *without* sacrificing your core principles.

Thus, you reach the apex of persuasive mastery—**negotiating with power.** You know how to set the stage, maintain a balanced stance, mirror emotional cues, make strategic concessions, escalate pressure when warranted, and exit gracefully. You do so with your conscience intact, your relationships stronger, and your deals documented. That is a far cry from a mere handshake in a dusty border outpost or a back-alley arrangement riddled with suspicion. This is the domain where legitimate authority meets undeniable influence, the realm of unshakable confidence and unwavering respect.

As we continue our journey, keep these negotiation lessons in your pocket. They will recur time and again, whether you're forging business alliances, mediating personal disputes, or striking deals at the edges of your comfort zone. Embrace the quiet power of words—*the gentlest chains, indeed*—and watch how gracefully the world bends to meet them. For once you master negotiation from both the criminal's cunning and the lawyer's discipline, few doors remain closed, and few minds remain impenetrable.

> "Speak softly yet with purpose, and the world will lean in to listen. Demand with care, and they will offer more than you dared to expect."

7
Building a Defense

> "Every move you make should leave no fingerprints."

A soft drizzle tapped against the hotel room's single window, the late-night sky broken only by flickering neon signs and the occasional headlights of passing cars. A man sat at a small wooden table, methodically flipping through pages of carefully gathered documents. Frayed edges, faded print, hastily scrawled notes—all evidence of his frantic attempts to piece together a fortress of paperwork. From time to time, he paused to jot down an additional thought or highlight a line of text. Upon closer inspection, you might have noticed that these "documents" were a mixed bag of official records, typed statements, and unassuming grocery receipts—each meticulously collected to serve a singular purpose: *self-protection.*

The man wore the tense, haunted look of someone juggling secrets. If questioned, he might have said he was just your average traveling salesman, or perhaps a consultant on the road for business. In truth, he was knee-deep in orchestrating a complex series of transactions that edged dangerously close to fraud. For weeks, he had posed as a legitimate liaison for a shadowy offshore firm, expertly dodging direct questions and presenting the illusion of respectable commerce. Now, he sensed scrutiny creeping closer. *Auditors were rummaging through financial statements.* A rival competitor was dropping hints that they "knew" more than they were letting on. The man had reason to fear that, unless he fortified his position, he risked being exposed—and possibly prosecuted.

In that dimly lit hotel room, he was effectively building his *defense.* While criminals typically operate in the shadows, always one step from the brink, a thoughtful portion of their energy goes into planning ways to shield themselves from the legal and social repercussions of their actions. Meanwhile, ethical professionals—from executives to lawyers—develop defenses of an entirely different caliber, using legitimate tools like documentation, contingency plans, and carefully crafted narratives that align with the truth. Yet the underlying principles, ironically, can be strikingly similar: *prepare exhaustively, assume the worst, and create a narrative so consistent that challengers struggle to find faults.*

In this chapter, we shift our focus to *Building a Defense.* Whether you're a high-stakes gambler in the underworld of con artistry or a law-abiding individual who needs to protect a business venture, understanding how criminals and lawyers gird themselves for worst-case scenarios offers vital lessons. You'll see how the cunning of a criminal merges seamlessly with the structured thoroughness of a seasoned attorney, revealing a method to fend off chaos, accusations, or catastrophes with the calm confidence of someone who has already charted every possible route of escape.

Defense as a Mindset—Expecting the Unexpected

> Prepare as if the threat looms around every corner—even if you walk in broad daylight."

Criminals develop a survival instinct that prods them to question every move, every alliance, and every document. This reflex doesn't arise from paranoia alone (though paranoia can be part of it). Instead, it's the logical outcome of existing in a world where a single oversight—a forgotten email, a slip of the tongue, a contradictory story—can bring the entire enterprise crashing down. In short, criminals live with the conviction that trouble is never far off. Hence, they prepare accordingly.

Lawyers, while operating under different ethics and aims, share a parallel viewpoint. A skilled attorney contemplates not just how to win a case but how an argument might fail if new evidence emerges. They imagine the worst-possible scenario—a surprise witness,

Mapping Multiple Escape Routes

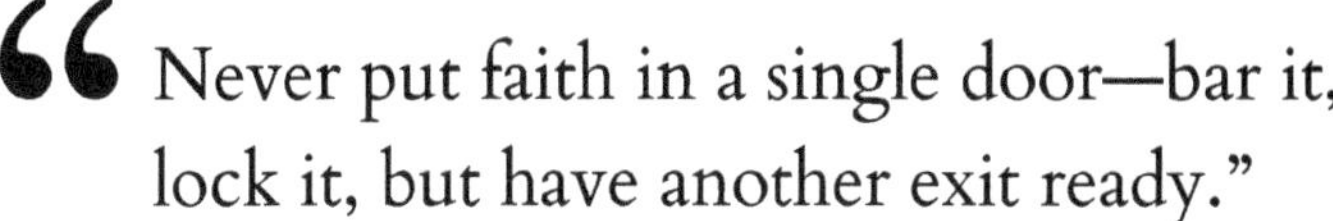

> "Never put faith in a single door—bar it, lock it, but have another exit ready."

The hallmark of a seasoned criminal is the presence of fallback plans. If the front entrance is compromised, they know a rear corridor leads to an alley. If a counterfeit passport fails, they've stashed another identity in a safe deposit box. If an accomplice grows unreliable, they can pivot to a different contact. This layered approach is not random; it's the outcome of meticulous planning, often including rehearsals of "Plan B" or even "Plan C."

In the legal sphere, attorneys embrace a parallel philosophy through *alternative pleading* and *backup arguments.* A complaint or defense can feature multiple lines of reasoning, each capable of standing on its own if another is struck down in court. If the judge disagrees with the first argument, the second or third might still prevail. Here, too, we see a layered defense strategy: never bet all on one outcome, especially in a realm rife with unpredictability.

In your everyday affairs, contingency planning can range from financial buffer funds to alternative suppliers in business, or simply having a second mentor lined up if your primary advisor isn't available. The lesson is that you should never assume a singular path will remain stable. Market conditions shift, people's attitudes change, technology fails. A well-structured defense means expecting these variations and designing a safety net that catches you before you fall too far.

Plausible Deniability

> “Deniability isn't about lying outright; it's about arranging facts so that no one can prove your intent.”

When criminals speak of *plausible deniability*, they refer to structuring operations so that if things go wrong, they can claim ignorance or frame their actions in an innocuous light. Maybe they never directly told the courier that the package contained illicit substances; they simply said, “Deliver this sealed bag.” Or they ensured that paperwork linked the suspicious funds to an entirely separate entity, creating distance between themselves and the incriminating details.

Lawyers leverage a similar principle when drafting clauses that limit a client's liability. It might be disclaimers in a contract (“The seller is not responsible for any unforeseen damages resulting from misuse of the product.”) or carefully worded statements that demonstrate a client's lack of knowledge or active wrongdoing. The goal is the same: *if trouble arises, can you plausibly claim you weren't aware, or that you exercised due diligence to the best of your abilities?*

In practical, lawful scenarios, plausible deniability can arise from well-documented disclaimers, transparent communication channels, and unambiguous roles and responsibilities. For example, if a business partner engages in unethical behavior, can you prove you had no part in that decision-making? Do your emails and meeting notes show that you raised concerns or were kept in the dark? That's the heart of plausible deniability. Though it should never be used to shirk genuine accountability, it's essential to recognize how a well-defined chain of authority and thorough documentation can shield you from fallout you never intended.

The Psychology of Preparation—Why We Often Fail to Defend Ourselves

> Complacency is the quiet assassin—lulling you into believing that danger lurks far from your doorstep."

Many people neglect defense-building until disaster looms. Why? Because proactive defense demands energy, resources, and a dose of healthy suspicion that can be mentally taxing. It's easier to trust that business partners will honor their word or that no one will scrutinize your financial records. Criminals, honed by necessity, rarely afford such naiveté. Lawyers, trained in the adversarial process, know that even an honest oversight can spell disaster in court.

Yet the rational mind must ask: *What is the cost of not preparing?* For criminals, the cost is often incarceration or a life on the run. For professionals or everyday individuals, it could mean lost business, tarnished reputation, or legal liability. Neglecting to build a defense is akin to leaving your front door unlocked in a high-crime neighborhood—sure, you might be fine for a while, but the risk is never truly minimal.

Embracing defense-building early can be liberating rather than stifling. Once you lay the groundwork—a robust paper trail, clear contracts, fallback options—you free yourself to focus on growth and creativity, confident that you have a fortress standing behind you should adversity strike.

The Art of Discretion

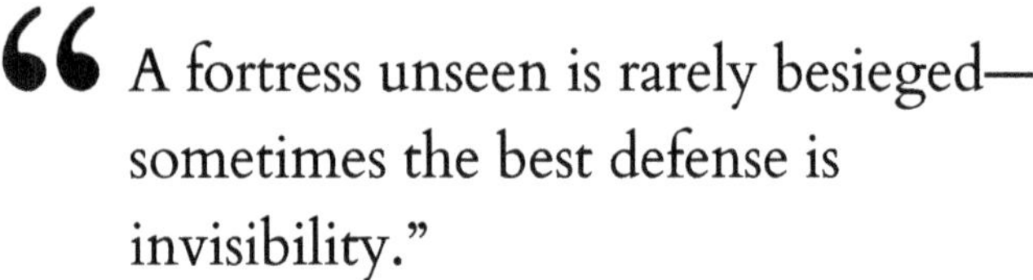

> "A fortress unseen is rarely besieged—sometimes the best defense is invisibility."

Sometimes, the most effective defense is to avoid attracting attention in the first place. Criminals who operate for years without getting caught often do so by staying under the radar—never flaunting sudden wealth, avoiding flashy purchases, and rotating locations or online profiles to prevent patterns from emerging. Lawyers similarly understand the value of discretion, especially in high-profile cases. They might negotiate deals behind closed doors, file motions under seal, or advise clients against public statements that can fuel gossip or speculation.

For you, discretion might mean selecting your confidants wisely, limiting how widely you share your strategic plans, and maintaining a social media presence that doesn't divulge sensitive details about your finances or business dealings. This doesn't imply paranoia; rather, it suggests *selective openness*. Share what's necessary, keep certain elements private, and ensure no easy trail leads unscrupulous individuals to your doorstep.

After all, if trouble does come knocking, the less it knows about you, the harder it is to mount a coordinated attack. This principle dovetails with our earlier discussions on reading the room and calculated risk: be aware of how much you reveal and to whom. When criminals gather intel, they love an open book. When lawyers strategize, they prefer to control the narrative that others see. The sweet spot lies in adopting both vantage points—knowing how to blend into the background even as you gather relevant information for your own needs.

A Staged Defense in Action

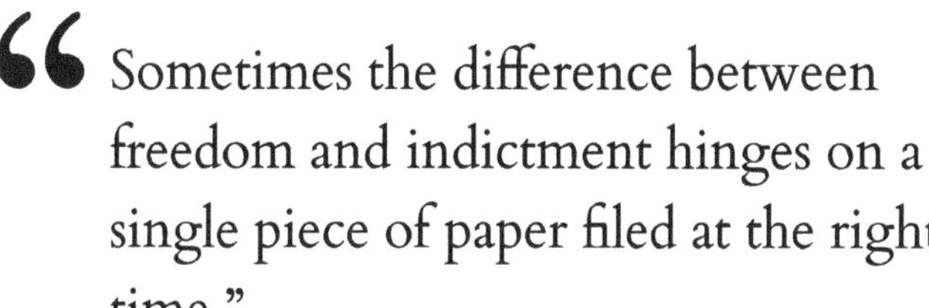

> "Sometimes the difference between freedom and indictment hinges on a single piece of paper filed at the right time."

Imagine a small company facing allegations of patent infringement by a larger, more established competitor. The CEO of the smaller firm, suspecting that trouble was brewing, had begun building a defense months earlier. They preserved every design sketch, timestamped every development meeting, and secured official receipts for each prototype to demonstrate an independent creation timeline predating the competitor's claim. They also had an outside expert ready to testify that the final product derived from a unique concept, not a rehashed or stolen idea.

When the lawsuit finally landed, the larger competitor expected a swift victory, hoping to intimidate the smaller company into a quiet settlement. Instead, they encountered a meticulously organized set of documents, precise engineer testimonies, and an external witness recognized in the industry. Confronted with overwhelming evidence, the bigger firm's legal team began to question the viability of their own claims, worried about losing both the case and public face. A settlement quickly emerged—not out of generosity, but out of strategic retreat.

The result was a textbook example of a *staged defense*. It didn't rely on deception or hidden agendas. Rather, it leveraged foresight, documentation, expert validation, and a narrative arc that was set in motion well before any lawsuit was filed. That same approach, albeit with a more clandestine twist, is mirrored by criminals who anticipate law enforcement's scrutiny and by attorneys defending clients against a barrage of civil or criminal charges. It is, at its core, the art of preparing for a storm while the skies are still clear.

Layering Your Defenses

> A single shield can shatter; a layered defense makes you impervious to most attacks."

In contemporary life, threats can emerge from multiple angles—litigation, reputational damage on social media, regulatory audits, or even internal betrayals by disgruntled colleagues. That's why a robust defense isn't a one-note strategy. It's a network of protections that reinforce each other.

- **Documentation** is your baseline, giving you the paper (or digital) proof of your actions.
- **Contingency plans** serve as your "what if" routes, ensuring you aren't cornered by unexpected changes.
- **Plausible deniability** keeps you insulated if associates or partners cross ethical lines.
- **Discretion** reduces the chances of attracting hostile attention in the first place.

Criminals have honed this layering technique to protect themselves at every turn, from building fake online identities to compartmentalizing activities so that no single person knows the entire operation. Lawyers employ parallel layering in case strategy, structuring each argument to stand independently so that if one fails, the rest hold the structure upright.

For you, layering might look like combining non-disclosure agreements with well-documented project timelines, a crisis communication plan, and a network of alliances that can vouch for your integrity. The synergy of these elements creates an environment where an adversary finds no easy target and must overcome multiple barricades to undermine you. In many cases, that alone discourages them from even trying.

Internal Discipline

> "A fortress is only as strong as the loyalty and diligence of those guarding its gates."

Criminals are all too aware that a single loose-lipped accomplice can unravel an entire operation. They practice internal discipline: limiting knowledge of the full plan, relying on loyalty forged through shared secrets or mutual benefit, and swiftly dealing with anyone who deviates. Lawyers, in a legitimate sphere, encourage discipline within an organization through clear policies, consistent messaging, and training sessions on compliance.

In any group endeavor, whether a fledgling startup or a long-established corporation, *the team is your immediate shield—or your most glaring vulnerability.* You can lock down documents, set up firewalls, and draft impressive contracts, but if an employee or partner leaks sensitive data or commits a breach of trust, your entire defense may crumble. Thus, part of building a defense is cultivating an internal culture of professionalism, confidentiality, and vigilance. Everyone must understand the stakes and adhere to agreed-upon protocols.

Criminals, ironically, excel at incentivizing loyalty. They often create a tight-knit environment where betrayal equals personal peril. Ethical enterprises don't need threats of violence, but they do need a robust sense of shared mission and trust that deters opportunistic betrayals. Clear procedures, open communication channels, and fair treatment can go a long way in ensuring that no one on your team has cause or desire to sabotage the collective effort.

When All Fails—The Art of Legal Surrender

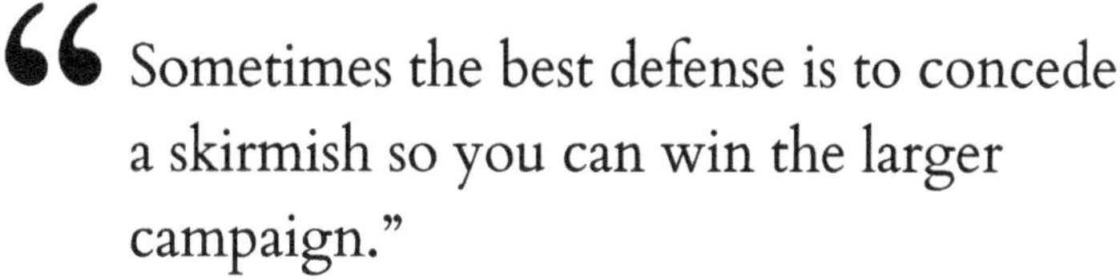

Despite our best precautions, sometimes the tide is too strong. Even well-prepared criminals face arrest, and even the most diligent lawyers occasionally meet a case that can't be salvaged with any brilliance of argument. In such circumstances, understanding *how* to surrender can be the key to preserving future possibilities.

A criminal might negotiate a plea deal, giving up lesser co-conspirators to gain leniency and reduce the years behind bars. An attorney, seeing an imminent loss, may advise a client to settle out of court or accept a plea to minimize prison time or financial liability. In both instances, the principle is the same: *save what can be saved.*

For you, that might mean accepting a partnership's dissolution to avoid a costly legal battle that could drain resources for years. Or it could entail resigning from a position where you're under intense scrutiny, preserving your reputation and leaving the door open for future re-entry into the field. Knowing when to cut your losses is not cowardice—it's strategic humility, acknowledging that your fortress cannot withstand this particular assault.

Once the storm passes, you can rebuild stronger than before.

A Final Reflection

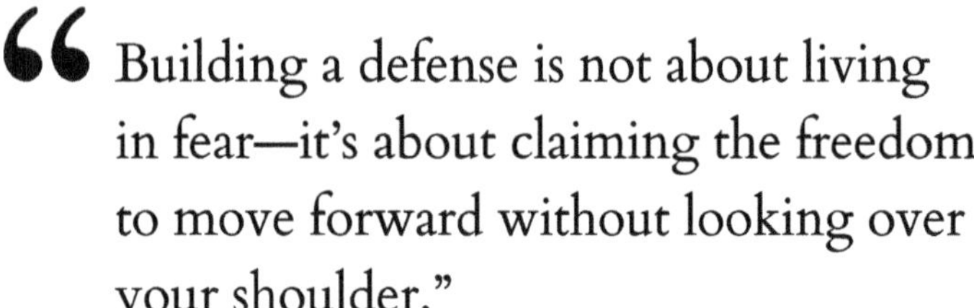

> "Building a defense is not about living in fear—it's about claiming the freedom to move forward without looking over your shoulder."

The criminals' perspective on preparation and lawyers' emphasis on thorough, well-structured strategies converge in the concept of *defensive mastery*. You've seen how anticipating trouble, maintaining records, crafting contingency plans, and upholding plausible deniability form the backbone of an ironclad shield. You've also recognized that this shield can be used ethically and transparently, so long as you remain anchored in honesty and professional conduct.

Remember, *defense* isn't purely about preventing legal battles or escaping blame. It's a mechanism that grants you peace of mind. When you know you've taken steps to verify your actions, secure your agreements, and foresee potential pitfalls, you can channel your energy into productive work. You become less reactive, less anxious, and better poised to seize opportunities because you're not weighed down by the dread of vulnerabilities lurking in the corners.

In the chapters to come, we'll pivot to the deeper intricacies of how to blend criminal cunning with legal prowess in the broader sphere of hustling—constructing alliances, moving invisibly under the radar, and ultimately managing power without letting it consume you. For now, let this chapter stand as your blueprint for resilience. A well-built defense isn't just about warding off threats; it's about ensuring your efforts, ambitions, and relationships aren't demolished by a single, unforeseen blow.

In the world of overlapping shadows and bright courtroom lights, *every move you make should indeed leave no fingerprints.* Whether you're forging ahead with a new business or defending a cherished cause, do so knowing that each step is part of a carefully wrought plan—a plan that, if challenged, can withstand scrutiny and protect all you've worked to achieve.

> "Fortify your life with foresight, and never fear the unexpected knock on your door. That is the essence of building an unassailable defense."

8

Mastering the Art of Persuasion

> "Win hearts, and minds will follow. Win minds, and hearts might never forget."

The courtroom sat in a hush that seemed to press itself against the very walls, as though the building were bracing for the words that would soon echo within its confines. Rows of weary spectators—family members, curious onlookers, a smattering of journalists—waited with a tangle of anticipation. At the front stood a lawyer known for his almost supernatural ability to sway even the most stubborn jury. He was not particularly tall or imposing, and his movements were measured, almost subdued. But when he spoke, the air charged with electricity.

That morning, he was representing a defendant accused of a serious financial crime. The evidence stacked high like an impregnable fortress, and the prosecution's cross-examination had been unrelenting. Most observers believed the verdict would be swift and damning. Yet in this final moment—the closing argument—something changed. The defense lawyer reached for a simple folder on the table, held it before the jury, and began: *"This folder is just paper and ink, yet it has the power to condemn an innocent man—or spare him. How we interpret its contents depends on more than facts; it depends on our shared humanity."*

Over the next twenty minutes, he moved seamlessly from earnest sincerity to rigorous logic, weaving the defendant's story into a tapestry of relatable struggles and overlooked details. By the time he concluded, several jurors dabbed at the corners of their eyes, while others bore pensive expressions. The prosecuting attorney, once so certain of victory, now felt something akin to vertigo—*the ground beneath the case was shifting*. That is the power of *persuasion* at its finest, an alchemy of emotional appeal and sharp reason, all bound together by an air of moral credibility.

This chapter zeroes in on how you, too, can tap into that transformative power of persuasion—a force criminals have manipulated for centuries to escape scrutiny, and lawyers have harnessed ethically to champion their clients. No matter your walk of life—whether you're a business leader, an artist, a negotiator, or simply a friend trying to resolve a conflict—*persuasion* can turn a stalemate into a breakthrough, a doubter into an ally, and an accusation into an opportunity for redemption.

Persuasion—The Silent Monarch of Human Interaction

> One does not rule by force alone; the smooth current of words can overthrow even the hardest walls."

Criminals have long recognized that raw power or brute force only goes so far. A well-placed bribe, a tearful plea, a charismatic lie—these often open doors that mere intimidation cannot. Likewise, lawyers undergo rigorous training in rhetorical techniques and debate strategies precisely because the law is not just about statutes; it's about *convincing* judges, juries, and even opposing counsel of a particular interpretation of those statutes. The criminals and attorneys who excel are those who understand that persuasion is not an optional flourish; it is *the bedrock of influence.*

In day-to-day life, we see persuasion in action constantly. A child cajoles a parent for a later bedtime with an invented sob story. An employee carefully frames an email to a boss, emphasizing how a new idea aligns with the company's objectives. Lovers promise each other change and devotion, forging new paths in relationships that might otherwise stagnate. Beneath every single one of these scenarios, persuasion is the quiet monarch—softly dictating the outcome without ever needing to announce its dominion.

Ethos—Credibility That Calms Doubt

> "If your voice wavers, your truth is overshadowed. Build your aura before building your argument."

In the realm of classical rhetoric, *Ethos* refers to the trustworthiness or credibility of the speaker. Criminals who manage to blend seamlessly into society capitalize on a deceptive ethos—perhaps by donning a pilot's uniform or forging impeccable credentials. Lawyers who sway a jury often do so by appearing above reproach, showcasing a polished confidence that reassures the court.

Credibility is not just about honesty—*it's about presentation.* A con artist who impersonates a surgeon doesn't begin by detailing advanced medical procedures; they start with a crisp white coat, a steady handshake, and an air of self-assured calm that stifles questions before they arise. Once people sense authority or expertise, they are more inclined to listen without immediate resistance.

To cultivate a powerful ethos in your personal or professional negotiations, consider how you project yourself. Are you well-prepared with data? Do you dress in a manner that instills respect? Do you speak with clarity, enunciating your points without wavering in tone? More importantly, do you *live* in a manner consistent with your words, so that those who know you can vouch for your integrity? Credibility is like a shield—when brandished correctly, it can deflect skepticism before it grows into outright opposition.

Pathos—Stirring Emotions to Speak Louder Than Logic

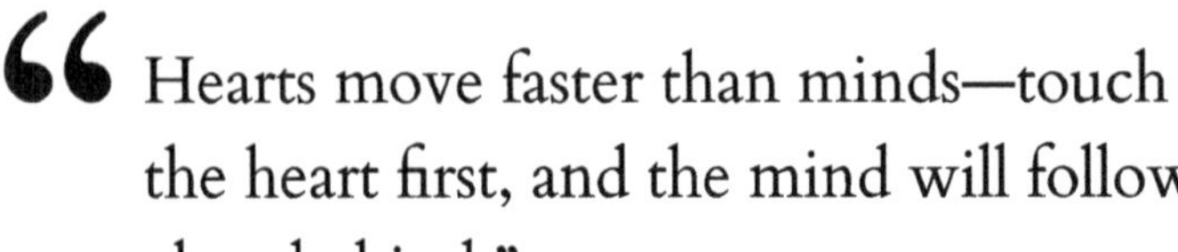

> "Hearts move faster than minds—touch the heart first, and the mind will follow close behind."

Pathos aims at the emotions. In a criminal's world, emotional manipulation can take many forms: a sob story that elicits pity, a threat that sparks fear, or a carefully orchestrated performance that conjures empathy. In the courtroom, skilled attorneys also wield pathos, painting vivid scenarios that place jurors into the emotional shoes of a defendant, or reminding them of a victim's suffering. Emotions, after all, are the undercurrent driving much of human decision-making, often overshadowing pure logic.

However, emotional appeal must be calibrated. Too much sentimentality can come off as contrived or manipulative. Too little leaves the listener cold, uninvested in the outcome. The trick lies in conjuring just enough emotional resonance to *open* the mind of the audience, making them more receptive to the factual arguments that will soon follow.

In everyday persuasion, be it a sales pitch or a heart-to-heart talk, pathos might involve sharing a personal anecdote or painting a vivid picture of what success or resolution could feel like. It could be as simple as letting genuine excitement shine through when discussing a project, or as solemn as recalling a painful lesson learned. When the listener feels a genuine emotional connection, they become a partner in the conversation rather than an adversary.

Logos—The Architecture of Rational Argument

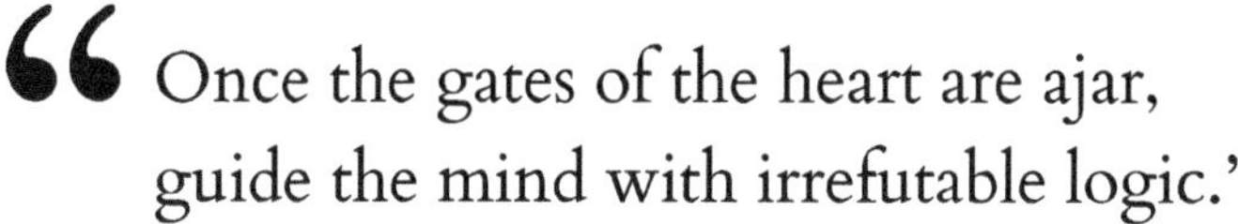

While emotions stir hearts, *logos*—the logical structure of an argument—cements one's case. Criminals who rely on persuasion mix in half-truths, plausible timelines, and carefully curated facts to build a story that stands up to cursory scrutiny. An imposter claiming to be a military veteran, for instance, might casually reference specific deployments or well-known commanding officers, layering enough detail to appear credible.

In court, attorneys carry entire binders of evidence, charts, and timelines, meticulously choreographed to support a particular narrative. This is logos in action: a systematic presentation of data and reasoning that draws a line from premise to conclusion so smoothly that listeners barely notice the journey.

Yet logos isn't just about burying people under spreadsheets or references; it's about clarity. A compelling argument is one that the average person, or juror, can follow without confusion. Punctuate points with real-life examples, analogies, or concise summaries. The objective is to remove any doubt that might remain after ethos and pathos have laid the groundwork.

In practical life, logos might take the form of a well-structured proposal at work, where you break down cost-benefit analyses, potential risks, and contingency plans. It might also be the simple, logical reasoning you lay out when negotiating a household budget. Once your listeners trust you (ethos) and resonate with your message (pathos), your logic (logos) can crystallize their agreement.

The Persuasion Trinity—Weaving Ethos, Pathos, and Logos

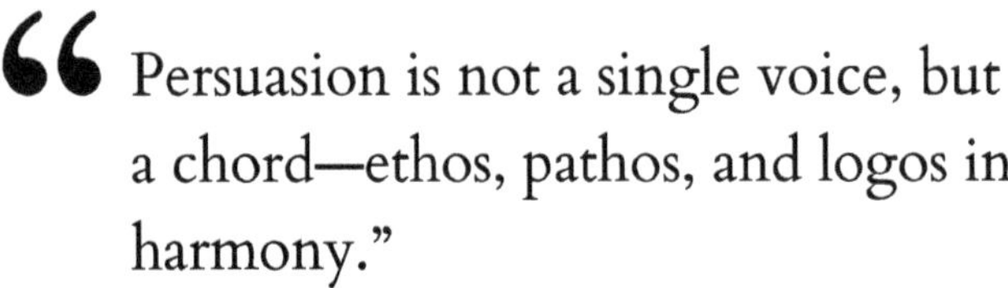

All three rhetorical pillars—ethos, pathos, and logos—are most effective when entwined. A con man might adopt a confident posture (ethos), deliver a heartfelt story of financial desperation (pathos), and back it up with fabricated but seemingly verifiable documents (logos). In a more legitimate context, a politician who aims to pass a crucial bill might begin by establishing their credibility and track record (ethos), stoke the public's emotional investment in the issue (pathos), and then outline the clear, logical benefits of the new legislation (logos).

The synergy of these elements is what propels persuasion from mere conversation to transformative dialogue. The crucial caveat, however, remains *ethics*. Criminals use these tools for personal gain at the expense of unsuspecting individuals or institutions. Lawyers and ethical professionals strive to employ them in the service of truth, justice, or collaborative benefit. The line between manipulation and genuine persuasion often hinges on intent.

Thus, as you refine your own approach to persuasion, reflect not just on how to harness these rhetorical tools but also on *why* you are doing so. If your aim is to produce a positive outcome—whether for your team, your client, or society at large—then sincerity and fairness should guide every step.

Influencing Bosses, Clients, and Even Adversaries

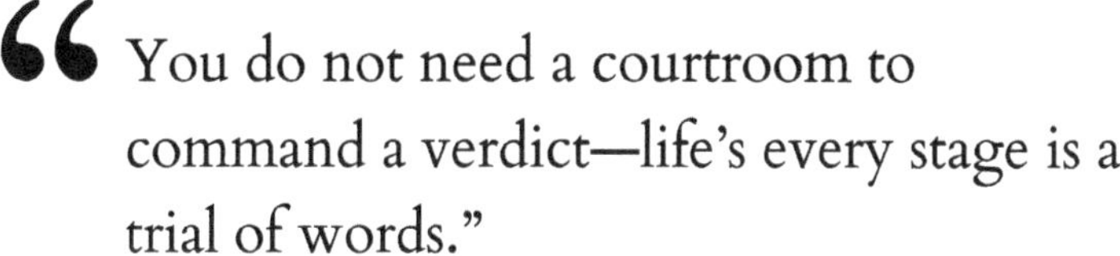

Influencing your boss: Suppose you're angling for a promotion. Rather than bombard your manager with demands, blend ethos, pathos, and logos. Establish credibility by highlighting your consistent performance and team contributions (ethos). Spark empathy by conveying how this growth aligns with shared organizational goals or how you've sacrificed personal time for the company's benefit (pathos). Finally, present a logical breakdown of the added value you bring, backed by metrics that confirm your success isn't just anecdotal (logos).

Dealing with clients: In a sales meeting, an effective persuader never just rattles off product features. They open by reassuring the client that they understand their industry challenges, citing relevant experience (ethos). Then they illustrate the emotional impact of resolving those challenges—reduced stress, greater pride in one's work (pathos). Lastly, they lay out precise data—cost savings, implementation timelines, return on investment (logos)—to seal the deal.

Negotiating with adversaries: Even in a confrontational setting, a calm display of credibility (ethos) can defuse tension before it escalates, showing you're neither intimidated nor antagonistic. A well-placed anecdote or respectful acknowledgment of the other side's concerns taps into empathy (pathos), reducing friction. Then you pivot to the undeniable logic of the situation (logos), outlining why collaboration or a mutually acceptable compromise is the superior path.

In every instance, persuasion is not about trickery. At its best, it's an invitation for others to see a shared vision—one that balances rational clarity with heartfelt resonance, anchored by a sense of trust in the persuader's character.

Lessons for the Ethical Persuader

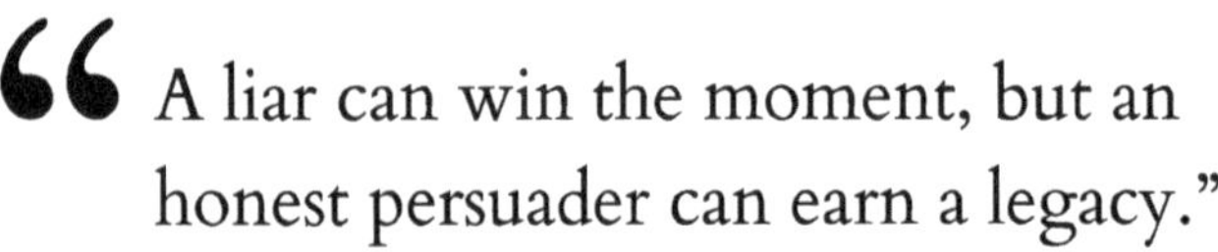

Criminals excel at reading vulnerabilities and crafting narratives that ensnare the unsuspecting. Lawyers, adept at professional advocacy, refine these same narrative skills within the boundaries of law and ethics. The criminal-lawmaker synergy suggests that persuasion is a *discipline*, not merely a gift of gab. It requires observing your audience closely, discerning their fears and desires, then packaging your message so it resonates on multiple levels.

Yet, you must remember that *the power to persuade can corrupt*. If you find yourself crossing lines—omitting vital truths, exaggerating facts beyond recognition, or preying on emotional weaknesses to manipulate someone into a decision that harms them—take a step back. Persuasion, wielded ethically, should leave you and your counterpart feeling that the outcome is both beneficial and respectful.

A lawyer stands by the principle that persuasion must operate on a bedrock of honesty and accountability. Even the best arguers in the courtroom cannot fabricate evidence without facing severe penalties. In everyday life, you are your own arbiter. You may slide into manipulation if you lose sight of moral bearings. But if you hold tight to ethical standards, you transform persuasion into a force that aligns with justice, progress, and meaningful collaboration.

Elevating Your Persuasive Arsenal

> “Influence, like a garden, flourishes through careful cultivation—water it with understanding, fertilize it with facts, and protect it with principle.”

While criminal tactics sometimes illuminate how humans can be manipulated, let these insights guide you toward a more conscientious use of persuasion. Study human behavior—notice what sparks enthusiasm in your colleagues, what calms agitation in a tense family discussion, what reassures a nervous client. Use that insight to shape your ethos, pathos, and logos approaches, never forgetting that sincerity fortifies every argument you present.

Reading widely and observing master persuaders—whether they are courtroom attorneys, seasoned politicians, or even revered public speakers—can sharpen your instinct. Practice summarizing complex data into digestible, logical arguments. Challenge yourself to deliver emotionally resonant stories. Above all, nurture your credibility by consistently acting with integrity, so people come to trust your words before you even speak.

In forging your unique style of persuasion, remember the confluence of cunning and law that underpins this book. The cunning mind identifies angles, unspoken motives, and emotional levers. The legal mind ensures that your approach respects ethical boundaries and stands on solid evidence. Merge these perspectives, and you become an influencer whose voice carries weight in every conversation—someone who understands that *real power* emerges when hearts and minds converge in agreement.

Toward Ethical Mastery

> "Persuasion done right opens doors for all; done wrong, it leads only to locked rooms and regret."

The ability to sway opinions, guide decisions, and shape outcomes is no trivial skill. Criminals often abuse this skill, while lawyers refine and regulate it. You, walking the delicate line between cunning and legality, can transform persuasion into a hallmark of leadership rather than a tool of manipulation.

As we proceed deeper into the broader tapestry of the *Criminal Mindset*, carry this understanding of persuasion with you. In subsequent chapters, we'll delve into the *Hustler's Playbook*, exploring how boundary-setters and alliance-builders harness persuasive prowess to navigate the labyrinth of power dynamics. Meanwhile, keep practicing. Catch yourself the next time you're about to press a point—*are you leaning too heavily on raw facts without emotional resonance? Are you presenting yourself credibly? Are you acknowledging the other side's legitimate concerns?* Integrate those self-checks, and watch as your influence expands.

Remember that the best persuaders are seldom the loudest. They often speak softly, but with words honed to a fine edge. They do not speak solely to win; they speak to unite, to inspire, and to clarify what might otherwise remain ambiguous or misunderstood. Where criminals sow discord, you can sow consensus. Where a manipulator tears down trust, you can build it. That is the essence of *Mastering the Art of Persuasion*—not merely securing agreement, but doing so in a way that leaves all parties stronger for having listened.

> In the final reckoning, true persuasion is not what you achieve but how you guide others to see a shared truth they never recognized before."

PART III

The Hustler's Playbook

9

The Rules of Engagement

> "The greatest hustler is the one who lets others believe they're in control."

The smoky smell of a busy nightclub lingered in the air, even though the establishment was shuttered during the daytime. A single overhead light illuminated the main area, revealing sticky floor tiles, a scattering of barstools, and a wide stage that looked eerily vacant. No customers were present, no music pulsated from hidden speakers. Instead, just two individuals stood in silent negotiation: a promoter who planned lucrative after-hours parties and a local organizer with ties to the city's underbelly. Both believed the other to be holding the final key to a profitable arrangement. Both saw an opportunity to bend the rules to their advantage.

They exchanged few words. Their posture said it all. The organizer seemed relaxed but mentally alert, as though each second was a chess move to evaluate. The promoter, flipping a pen through his fingers, eyed the dusty corners of the club and the unseen potential it held. They discussed security fees, liquor permits, and *potential issues* that needed careful handling. In this charged atmosphere, they each played by an invisible set of guidelines—rules of engagement—that governed how hustlers and opportunists broker deals on the edge of law and order.

That tableau offers a glimpse into the *hustler's world*: a realm where formal contracts often yield to unspoken codes, and where sincerity coexists with cunning in an unpredictable dance. This chapter, *The Rules of Engagement*, extends beyond the standard definitions of negotiation. It delves into the unspoken protocols that criminal masterminds and legitimate powerbrokers alike observe when entering alliances, forging plans, or orchestrating hustles. By understanding these unspoken rules, you can navigate ethically complicated landscapes with both confidence and caution, ensuring that you remain *in command* of each situation rather than a naive player at the mercy of sharper minds.

The Hustler's Domain

> "Blurred lines aren't violations; they're opportunities—if you know how to tread carefully."

The hustler's world is rarely black or white. Instead, it's an expanse of grays where legal paperwork mingles with handshake deals, and moral compasses can spin unpredictably. Criminals thrive here, exploiting legal loopholes and social blind spots. Entrepreneurs, too, often find themselves in gray zones—experimenting with new business models, forging alliances in uncharted markets, or capitalizing on fleeting gaps in regulations. In each scenario, the hustler moves forward by *sensing* these ambiguities and turning them into avenues for potential gain.

But here's the crucial distinction: *observing the rules of engagement* is what separates the savvy operator from the reckless gambler. In a gray-zone negotiation, misunderstandings and betrayals can erupt at any moment, so hustlers evolve their own brand of etiquette. They know how to read signals of trust or distrust, and how to adjust their approach before a deal falls apart or escalates into conflict.

For you, stepping into this domain doesn't mean you must abandon ethical practices. Rather, it means recognizing that most high-stakes deals, whether in business or diplomacy, have layers of nuance that extend beyond a written contract. Being aware of those subtle signals, cultural norms, and unspoken bargains can help you orchestrate outcomes more effectively—and with fewer unpleasant surprises.

Rule 1

Always Offer a Perception of Control

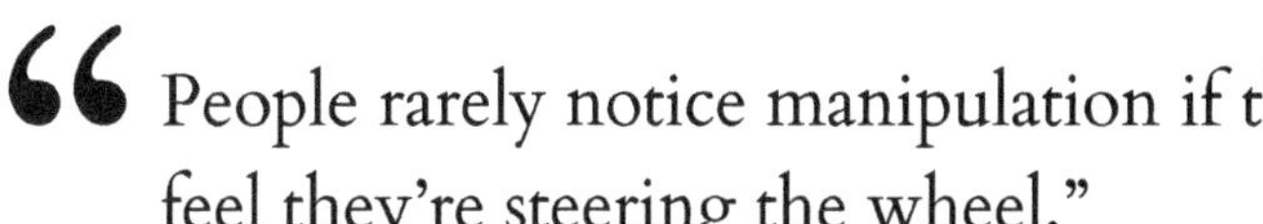

> "People rarely notice manipulation if they feel they're steering the wheel."

Criminals, con artists, and hustlers of all stripes deploy a critical tactic when forging pacts: they let the other party *believe* they have the upper hand. By encouraging this illusion, they distract from the carefully hidden strings they've woven beneath the surface of the agreement. It's a magic trick of sorts: *pay attention to this grand gesture while the real move happens elsewhere.*

In a more legitimate setting, letting others feel in control works wonders too. An astute business negotiator might say, "You're free to structure the payment plan in a way that suits your budget," knowing full well they've already set an agenda for the final numbers. A skilled project manager might invite employees to propose deadlines, gently steering them to choose a timeline already in mind.

This principle of perceived control fosters collaboration rather than resentment. People are far more agreeable when they think a plan was their idea. This approach does not necessitate deceit or unethical behavior; it simply recognizes that *self-importance* can be a powerful motivator. Let a colleague or partner relish their sense of input, and they become far less inclined to obstruct your overarching goals.

Rule 2

Never Reveal Your Full Hand

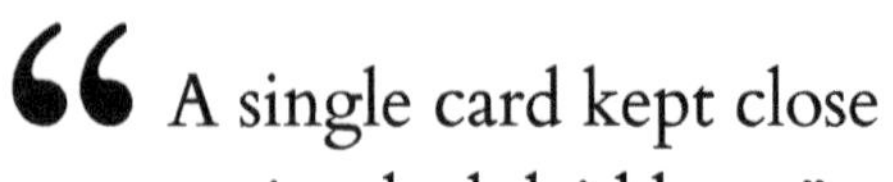

A single card kept close can trump an entire deck laid bare."

Whether you're a pickpocket caseing a crowded street or a corporate executive refining an acquisition bid, *information* is currency. Criminals hoard details about potential marks or adversaries, revealing as little as possible about themselves in return. The reason is simple: the less you disclose, the fewer angles someone else has to exploit you.

In legitimate contexts, you might think of it as cautious discretion. If you're negotiating a major deal, you don't show your bottom line at the outset; you hold back certain concessions or budget figures until the critical phase. In workplace dynamics, you don't broadcast every strategic thought to the entire team—some knowledge must be reserved for key allies or for moments when you need to solidify a point.

This rule dovetails with the earlier chapter on *Reading the Room*. The more you learn about others, and the less you hand over about your vulnerabilities, the sturdier your negotiating position becomes. This is not about deceit; it's about measured transparency. When you dole out information too freely, you risk losing the leverage that well-timed revelations can offer.

Rule 3

Study the Subtext, Not Just the Words

Hustlers don't hear the words spoken; they hear the intentions masked beneath them."

In the hustler's world, spoken promises or statements are frequently half-truths or placeholders. Criminals habitually say one thing while planning another. This is why the most successful hustlers pay greater attention to tone, pauses, and body language than to literal phrasing. They want to sense if there's an unspoken hesitation or an invisible line someone won't cross.

Even in respectable professional spheres, it's the subtext that can signal hidden agendas. A business partner who says, "We're open to collaboration," might be testing whether you'll overcommit to a compromised position. A politician declaring a broad policy goal could be gauging public reaction before revealing the fine print.

This underscores a recurring theme in this book: *awareness.* If you focus solely on the words, you miss half the conversation. Train yourself to observe the flicker of doubt in someone's eyes or the careful hedging in their statements—these minor cues often reveal whether a deal is truly on stable ground or if you're about to step into a carefully laid trap.

Rule 4

Barter with Value, Not Necessarily Morals

The hustler's handshake is currency. Morality is a moving target—value is tangible."

In underworld dealings, moral compasses rarely align, and trust is a fragile construct. What replaces moral conviction, then, is a raw sense of *value exchange.* Criminals learn to weigh whether a job is worth the risk and if an ally is worth the possible betrayal. This is why currency can take many forms: protection, insider knowledge, access to networks, or simply cash.

In legitimate negotiations, morals do play a larger role—you're not aiming to swindle or break the law. Yet the principle of value still holds supreme. A savvy negotiator asks, "What does the other side want so badly that they'll meet me halfway?" If you can pinpoint that desire—be it prestige, quick project turnaround, or social impact—you can trade it for what *you* need, without resorting to moral compromise.

By separating moral judgments from pragmatic value, you clarify what each party genuinely brings to the table. This clarity can help you create deals that feel fair, leaving both sides satisfied. Even when your morals remain intact, understanding value as a currency ensures you don't rely solely on good faith or intangible promises. You root your engagements in mutually beneficial exchanges that reduce the likelihood of exploitation.

Rule 5

Create Exit Routes, Then Decide If You Need Them

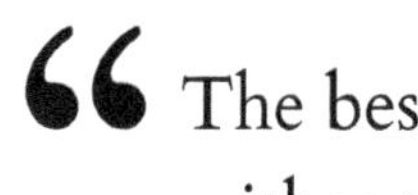

The best hustlers know how to vanish without a trace—yet often, the real power lies in choosing to stay."

In the hustler's playground, survival often depends on the ability to disappear at the first sign of danger. Criminals thrive on orchestrating fake identities and backdoor escapes—metaphorically and literally. If a deal goes sour, they can sever ties, slip into anonymity, and live to plot another day.

For aboveboard professionals, exit routes take the form of backup contracts, kill-fee clauses or dissolution agreements. They ensure that if a partnership disintegrates or the market takes a nosedive, you're not left bankrupt or powerless. Having such contingencies grants a psychological advantage: you negotiate from a position of *composed readiness*. If you need to pull out, you can do so without catastrophic losses.

However, paradoxically, when you know you *can* walk away, you may discover that staying in the deal and nurturing it is often more beneficial in the long run. This is where ethics and cunning converge—because sometimes the greatest act of power is not running from risk but choosing to keep forging ahead, secure in the knowledge that you have a safety net if all else fails.

Rule 6

Camouflage Yourself Strategically

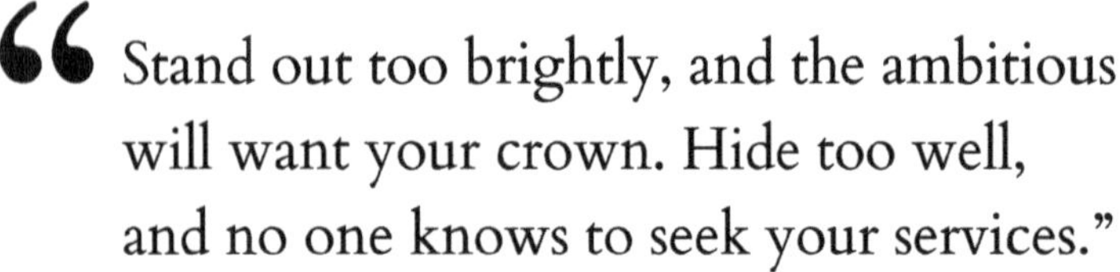

"Stand out too brightly, and the ambitious will want your crown. Hide too well, and no one knows to seek your services."

A central theme among hustlers is the art of camouflage. While criminals aim to avoid law enforcement, legitimate power-players also recognize the value of blending in to avoid envy or sabotage. Think of an entrepreneur who keeps a modest lifestyle despite significant wealth, evading the pitfalls of public envy. Or a new manager who quietly studies the workplace culture before asserting bold changes, to avoid instant backlash.

At the same time, you don't want to become invisible in a competitive environment. Ambition often demands at least a *calibrated* level of visibility. You might flash certain credentials or accomplishments when it can open doors, but remain humble or reticent about your true depth of resources until you're certain it's advantageous to reveal them.

This principle loops back to the concept of *never revealing your full hand.* Camouflaging your strengths until the moment is ripe can dissuade potential threats and allow you to observe the field without prematurely announcing your capabilities. Criminals do this instinctively; a well-prepared professional does it with calculated awareness.

Rule 7

Enforce Boundaries Quietly but Firmly

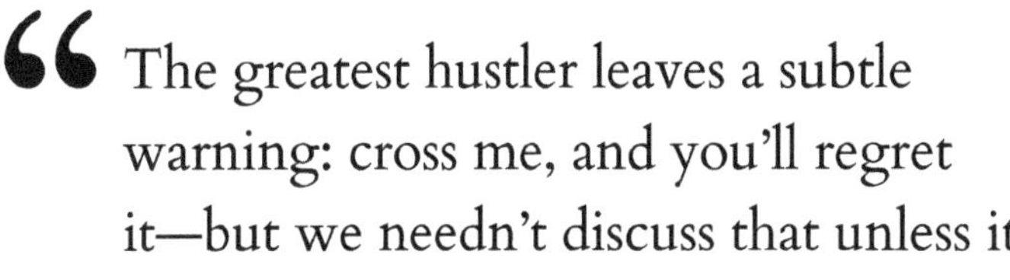

> "The greatest hustler leaves a subtle warning: cross me, and you'll regret it—but we needn't discuss that unless it becomes necessary."

The hustler's code demands that you protect your interests without resorting to constant displays of aggression. Criminals might rely on ominous reputations or cryptic hints that betrayal comes with dire consequences. Similarly, corporate moguls or senior attorneys can project firm boundaries by how they respond to small offenses—an immediate, composed correction that sets a precedent for future conduct.

The key is consistency. If you threaten consequences, you must be prepared to enact them when lines are crossed. Otherwise, your boundaries become empty talk. Yet these threats need not be overt. Often, a quiet word or a subtle reminder of one's capabilities works more effectively than an overt ultimatum. In many respects, this parallels the dynamic in nature where the most dangerous animals often do not roar incessantly; they simply make it clear that intruders risk a swift reprisal.

By maintaining quiet but unyielding boundaries, you let others know that while you prefer cooperation, you're not to be trifled with. This mixture of approachability and latent resolve cultivates respect more efficiently than constant posturing ever could.

Rule 8

Honor Among Thieves—Or at Least Among Partners

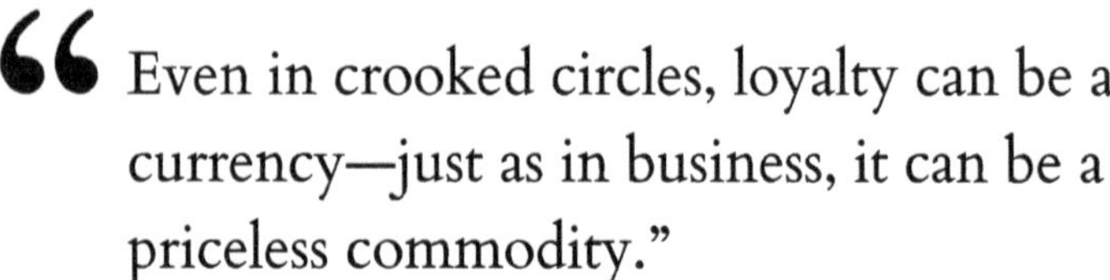

"Even in crooked circles, loyalty can be a currency—just as in business, it can be a priceless commodity."

Despite their willingness to bend or break laws, many successful criminals adhere to a form of *honor*. They understand that betraying allies or partners too frequently leads to isolation and, ultimately, downfall. Trust, even in murky environments, acts as social glue that keeps joint ventures running smoothly.

In legitimate endeavors, loyalty and trust are similarly vital. If your associates see you consistently undercutting them or wiggling out of obligations, they will sever ties at the first sign of trouble. Conversely, if you're known for honoring your word—even in difficult circumstances—you gain a reputation that can carry you through lean times. People will invest in relationships with you because they've heard the stories of your reliability.

This is not about naive idealism. Rather, it's a pragmatic observation: *trust is an asset that's hard to earn and easy to squander.* Criminals might take drastic steps to punish traitors, whereas in business you might simply walk away from someone who betrays you. Either way, understanding the value of honor—even if it's a more flexible version in these gray realms—helps you forge stable alliances that can withstand the inevitable storms.

Rule 9

Manage Perceptions, Publicly and Privately

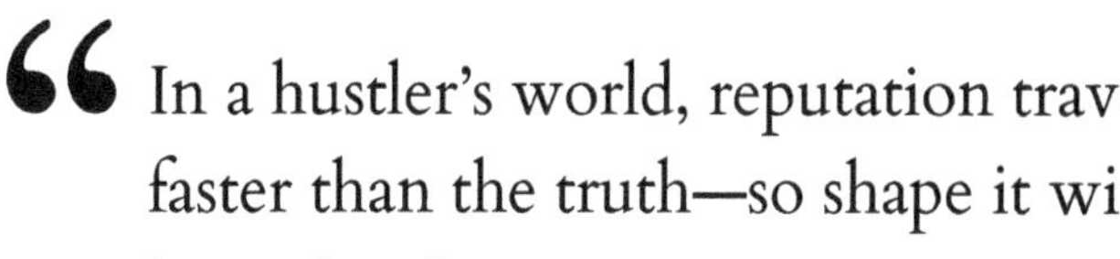

"In a hustler's world, reputation travels faster than the truth—so shape it with intention."

Criminal syndicates often cultivate carefully crafted public images. Some portray themselves as pillars of the community, funding local events or charities, thereby diverting suspicions from illegal activities. Corporate giants sponsor philanthropic campaigns, media appearances, and philanthropic awards, buffering criticism of their sometimes cutthroat practices. Both see the advantage of managing external perceptions.

In your world, this means being mindful of how you present yourself across multiple platforms: social media, community events, workplace conversations. If you want to be taken seriously in your field, ensure your LinkedIn profile or company website conveys expertise and consistent messaging. If rumors crop up about unethical behavior (whether true or not), address them directly rather than letting suspicion fester.

On a private level, be cautious about who you reveal personal details to—gossip can tarnish an image in ways that take years to rectify. Criminal or not, once your name is embroiled in negative perceptions, reacquiring credibility can be an uphill battle. Managing your reputation is an ongoing effort, not a one-time task.

The Common Thread—Fluid Morality in a Shifting Landscape

> “Rules bend in this domain—not necessarily from malice, but because adaptation often outpaces regulation.”

When criminals use the term *hustler*, they don’t always imply con artistry. They might reference anyone who operates quickly, seizes opportunities, and navigates uncertain waters with dexterity. In legitimate business, we call these people *innovators*, *market disruptors*, or *entrepreneurs*—those who see shifting regulations and evolving consumer demands as stepping stones rather than obstacles.

The hustler’s rules of engagement reflect a *fluid morality*: they adapt to the context at hand. If a certain hustle feels dangerously close to unscrupulous territory, a savvy hustler might recalibrate, deciding the short-term gain isn’t worth the long-term fallout. In ethical circles, this mirrors how conscientious leaders weigh the social implications of an aggressive expansion.

The lesson for you is to approach gray areas with eyes wide open. Whether your hustle is launching a groundbreaking app, forging a strategic partnership with a historically difficult colleague, or venturing into an emerging market that lacks stable regulations, apply these unwritten rules carefully. Seek alignment with your broader values, but don’t shy away from exercising caution, camouflage, or subtle boundary enforcement.

The Ethically Tuned Hustler

> A hustler with principles becomes unstoppable—unconstrained by fear and undefeated by cunning rivals."

By synthesizing these rules of engagement—perception of control, selective disclosure, reading subtext, bartering with value, strategic exits, controlled visibility, quiet boundaries, mutual honor, and mindful reputation management—you rise above naive players who rely solely on conventional rules and unimaginative tactics. You also transcend the blind risk-taking that characterizes shady deals with no safety net.

Most importantly, you fortify your own conscience in a domain where others let go of morality too easily. This doesn't mean you must walk the same line as a criminal or adopt underhanded methods. Quite the opposite. You wield these insights *to safeguard yourself from exploitation* and to create robust frameworks that support genuine, long-lasting success.

If criminals can flourish briefly using cutthroat strategies, imagine how much farther you can go by blending their cunning with moral backbone and legal savvy. You can outthink short-sighted hustlers, navigate daunting markets with agility, and broker alliances that benefit all parties—earning you a durable form of respect that criminals rarely enjoy.

In the next chapters, we'll continue unraveling the hustler's playbook, focusing on building alliances and staying under the radar—two core strategies that complement these rules of engagement. Stay sharp, remain open to nuanced opportunities, and remember that in the hustler's domain, those who quietly abide by an invisible code often end up shaping the game from behind the scenes.

> Rules exist everywhere—but in the hustler's world, it's the unwritten rules that shape destiny."

10
Building Alliances

> "Even the fiercest lone wolf knows the strength of the pack."

In the chilly predawn silence of an unnamed coastal city, two figures stepped onto a secluded pier. A dull orange glow from distant street lamps flickered across the water's surface, revealing the outlines of abandoned fishing boats rocking gently in the breeze. If you squinted, you could see a sleek black sedan parked a short distance away, its headlights off, engine idling. Neither of the two figures spoke as they approached an old warehouse looming at the edge of the pier.

They had come to broker an alliance. On the surface, it was a puzzling encounter: one was rumored to be affiliated with a local crime syndicate—someone known for back-room deals and contraband shipments.

The other wore the polished shoes and impeccable suit of a high-powered attorney who lived by the letter of the law. Their worldviews should have clashed like oil and water, yet here they were. A mutual threat had emerged from a rival group, and survival demanded collaboration.

In that moment—beneath the silent watch of the stars, with the smell of salt and gasoline lingering in the air—a subtle transformation took place. The two adversaries-turned-allies recognized a simple truth: *no matter how cunning a mastermind may be, no one conquers the game entirely alone.* Alliances, even the most unexpected ones, unlock doors that remain sealed to solitary operators.

This chapter, *Building Alliances*, investigates how criminals, lawyers, and anyone navigating a complex world of shifting loyalties can form bonds that amplify strength without forfeiting independence. Whether you're forging corporate partnerships, political coalitions, or personal friendships, understanding the art of alliance-building is essential. We'll peek into the underworld's code of loyalty, then pivot to the refined tactics attorneys employ in forging strategic pacts. Along the way, you'll glean methods to unify people behind a common cause—balancing caution with commitment so that both sides walk away more powerful than before.

Alliance—When One Plus One Becomes Three

An alliance is more than a handshake—it's a summation of shared vision and synchronized strengths."

A criminal ring thrives on alliances that supply safe houses, insider tips, or additional muscle. A single thief might be adept at picking locks, but a team comprised of hackers, getaway drivers, and corrupt officials opens the floodgates of possibility. Similarly, in a law firm, each attorney might specialize in a different niche—tax law, litigation, mergers. When these experts band together, they craft an airtight fortress of services that outmaneuvers any solo practitioner.

In simpler terms, alliances generate *synergy*. It's not just about dividing tasks; it's about merging talents so that you create an outcome greater than the sum of its parts. The lone wolf might boast a certain romantic appeal, but the hustler who can rally allies—who can establish networks that endure beyond a single transaction—inevitably wields a broader, more resilient influence.

Look at how con artists sometimes team up with lawyers (often unwittingly on the lawyer's part). The con artist might persuade unsuspecting victims to part with money, while the attorney, strictly within legal lines, handles the tangled aftermath. Neither alone could manage both the con and the cleanup. Combined, they weave a tapestry of plausible cover stories that can be alarmingly effective. These dark examples illuminate a universal principle: two specialized skills working in tandem can surpass any single, generalist skill.

The Hidden Contracts of Loyalty

> "In the underworld, deals are rarely written; they're etched into mutual necessity and sealed by caution."

Criminals who pool resources rarely bother with official paperwork. After all, *written contracts can become evidence.* Instead, they develop an internal ledger of obligations and favors. One gangster might loan weapons to another's crew, expecting loyalty in future turf disputes. The currency is trust—tempered by fear of betrayal's consequences.

Attorneys and legitimate professionals, by contrast, rely on meticulously drafted contracts. But even here, a deeper undercurrent of *unwritten obligation* runs parallel to the legal documents. When two law firms collaborate on a complex case, they might sign a joint venture agreement. Yet it's the personal rapport—the subtle signals of reciprocal respect—that truly cements the alliance. If the trust erodes, even the most ironclad written contract can splinter under the stress of acrimony.

In your own world, forging effective alliances means recognizing that both explicit and implicit agreements hold weight. Yes, put major points in writing to avoid confusion. But also pay attention to the intangible currency of honor, respect, and reciprocity. Those intangible threads often keep alliances stable when unforeseen crises—legal, personal, or financial—arise.

Strategic Alliances vs. True Partnerships

> “All alliances may share the same handshake, but some end with knives in the back.”

Not all alliances are built alike. *Strategic alliances* often prioritize short-term gains: criminals might pool manpower for one heist, then scatter once the job is done. Businesses might co-brand a product launch, then part ways as soon as the market test concludes. These alliances can be incredibly profitable but run high on uncertainty. If your ally sees an exit ramp that offers greater advantage, they'll likely take it with minimal remorse.

True partnerships, on the other hand, root themselves in long-term objectives. Think of two family-run companies merging decades of generational wisdom, or a law firm that absorbs a smaller practice to create a well-rounded legal powerhouse. Partnerships thrive on shared risk, shared vision, and a level of trust that transcends immediate profit. While strategic alliances can yield rapid returns, true partnerships become the bedrock of sustained success.

As you navigate your alliances, recognize which category you're falling into. Are you forging a fleeting, scenario-specific link? Then watch for signs of opportunism and guard your vital interests. But if you aim for a more enduring bond, invest extra time in building rapport and transparency. Clarify the shared mission. When both parties wholeheartedly believe in a mutual goal, betrayal becomes costlier and less appealing than loyalty.

Motives and Weaknesses—The Heart of Alliance-Building

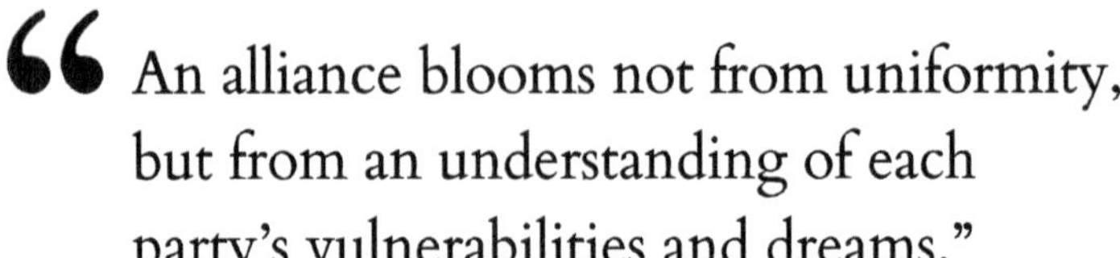

> “An alliance blooms not from uniformity, but from an understanding of each party’s vulnerabilities and dreams.”

Criminal masterminds meticulously research potential allies’ motives: Is it greed, desperation, or ambition that drives them? Which vulnerabilities can be exploited to ensure loyalty? For instance, a small-time smuggler might be grappling with personal debt, making him pliable to a bigger player who offers both quick cash and an escape route from creditors. In exchange, the smuggler provides local intel.

Lawyers, especially in negotiations, analyze what’s fueling their counterpart’s stance. Perhaps the other firm’s leadership is under pressure to show growth to investors, or maybe the client has personal reasons for settling quickly. By discerning these hidden motivations, a lawyer can craft an alliance (or settlement) that speaks directly to the other party’s core needs. That’s the essence of “win-win”—you scratch my back, I scratch yours, and we both walk away enriched.

However, never forget that acknowledging someone’s weakness doesn’t necessitate exploiting it unethically. The real artistry lies in offering solutions or resources that address the other side's concerns while strengthening your own position. *Mutual benefit is the golden thread* that keeps alliances from devolving into predatory relationships.

Balancing Trust and Wariness

> To open your gates is to invite an ally—or an invader—into your fortress. The difference is in your vigilance."

All alliances carry risks. Criminal rings worry about informants. Businesses fear intellectual property theft. Politicians guard against scandal if the alliance goes sour. Trust, then, must be carefully rationed. You can't lock down your castle entirely, or no ally would ever come in. But fling open the gates without due caution, and you risk sabotage.

Criminals mitigate this risk by restricting information flow—no single underling knows the full scope of a plan. Lawyers or executives use *non-disclosure agreements* and carefully negotiated terms to keep strategic secrets safe. Both are variations on the same principle: share enough to collaborate effectively, but withhold enough to retain autonomy if betrayal looms.

In your alliances, consider compartmentalizing knowledge. Reveal crucial data in increments, scaling trust as the relationship proves itself reliable. This approach not only safeguards your interests but also builds a sense of shared journey—if the ally meets each milestone of trust, the partnership deepens organically.

The Magnet of Shared Enemies

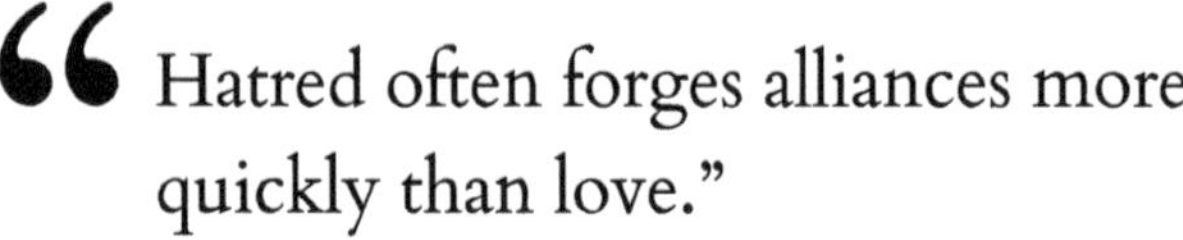

> "Hatred often forges alliances more quickly than love."

Criminal outfits regularly unite against a common threat: a rival gang muscling into their territory or a new law enforcement crackdown. The logic is primal: *if you and I do not band together, we'll both be devoured by a bigger beast.* In a more lawful context, two rival corporations might suspend their competition to challenge a new market disruptor. Or political factions might temporarily bury the hatchet to combat a mutual adversary in an election.

When forging alliances based on shared enemies, be mindful that such bonds can dissolve the instant the mutual threat diminishes. Indeed, after fending off the rival, your ally might revert to competing with you. If you're aiming for a stable, long-term relationship, shift the focus from defeating a shared enemy to achieving shared gains. Yet if immediate survival is the sole objective, then by all means exploit the galvanizing power of a common foe. Just keep an eye on the horizon, ready for shifting loyalties once the dust settles.

Rituals and Symbols—Cementing the Pact

> “A deal is more than terms—it’s also the moment of binding. Formal or not, symbols forge memory.”

Criminals sometimes stage dramatic ceremonies—blood oaths, coded tattoos, or clandestine gatherings—to seal a new alliance. While these rituals might appear theatrical, they reinforce a psychological bond. Similarly, legitimate organizations employ formal ceremonies: contract-signing events, ribbon-cuttings, press conferences. These public gestures solidify the partnership in the eyes of stakeholders, employees, or the broader community.

Why do rituals matter? Because humans thrive on *symbols*. A handshake, a toast, or even a notarized document can carry immense emotional weight, transforming a mere agreement into something sacred or official. When you create alliances in your professional or personal life, don’t skip that final symbolic step. It could be as small as meeting face-to-face over lunch or as elaborate as a partnership unveiling at a company gala. Either way, the memory lingers, reminding each party that they’ve not just agreed on terms, but also entered a relational pact worthy of respect.

Exiting Alliances Gracefully

> Every alliance has a season. The wise ally plans the farewell from the first hello.”

Not all alliances are forever. Criminal syndicates might dissolve after a lucrative run. Business mergers may unravel due to diverging visions. Even friendships can morph into polite distance once life circumstances shift. What separates a graceful exit from a chaotic implosion is foresight.

Criminals who anticipate an alliance's end might quietly shuffle resources elsewhere, ensuring no single partner can sabotage their entire operation. Lawyers include exit clauses in contracts: buyout options, distribution of assets, or severance terms. In personal alliances, open communication can soften the blow—explaining changes in priorities or goals, rather than abruptly ghosting the relationship.

If you cultivate your alliances with the awareness that parting ways might someday be necessary, you can *engineer* the exit to preserve mutual dignity. This approach protects reputations—yours and theirs—and keeps avenues open for future collaboration should circumstances realign. After all, burning bridges, especially in a world where circles tend to be tight-knit, can come back to haunt you.

The Syndicate and the Neighborhood

Sometimes the best alliance crosses the boundary between criminal and civil life—and both sides benefit."

Imagine a run-down neighborhood plagued by petty crime and drug trafficking. A local crime boss operates with tacit approval from certain residents who fear or respect him. Then enters a community organizer, desperate to reduce violence but lacking resources. At first glance, these two individuals should be mortal enemies: one embodies lawlessness, the other community welfare.

Yet a fragile alliance forms. The organizer recognizes that the crime boss's influence could forcibly curb certain out-of-control elements—particularly from outside gangs. The boss sees a chance to gain local favor, reducing heat from the police if the neighborhood's crime stats dip. A handshake emerges: The boss keeps external gangs at bay, the organizer channels municipal funds into legitimate local business development—ensuring stable jobs that reduce the likelihood of random street crime.

Are they solving the root problems? Not entirely. Is it moral to collaborate with a crime lord? Debatable. But from the vantage point of realpolitik, both sides see immediate benefits that overshadow moral quandaries. This *uneasy alliance* lowers violence, fosters some economic uptick, and fortifies the boss's local standing. Eventually, such an arrangement may unravel—perhaps the neighborhood organizes a more wholesome security plan, or the boss overreaches. But until that day, the alliance stands as a testament to how even sworn enemies can join forces under common interests.

Strengthening Your Alliance-Building Toolkit

> “People follow those who understand their fears, champion their hopes, and prove their reliability—words alone are never enough.”

Mastering alliance-building goes beyond memorizing a few guidelines. It demands emotional intelligence, ethical clarity, and consistent follow-through. Here are some practical moves:

- **Identify Core Motives:** Before approaching a potential ally, research what truly drives them. Is it status, security, financial gain, or altruism? Tailor your proposal to highlight how your alliance meets their root needs.
- **Set Clear Objectives:** Even if you're forging a fluid or short-term alliance, define success metrics. Criminals might want a certain profit margin, while corporate partners might aim for a percentage of market share. Shared goals reduce ambiguity.
- **Adopt Rituals:** Mark the formation of an alliance with a symbolic gesture—an agreement signing, an official statement, or a private, meaningful meeting. Psychologically, it helps both parties transition from casual talk to committed action.
- **Nurture the Relationship:** Stay in contact, share relevant updates, offer small gestures of goodwill. Don't wait for a crisis to test your bond.

- ▷ **Plan the Exit (Quietly):** Even if you foresee a lifelong partnership, keep a blueprint for parting ways amicably. Whether it's a formal buyout clause or a simple "Let's revisit our arrangement every quarter," clarity about the future wards off nasty surprises.

Remember, criminals operate with minimal regulation, yet still manage to forge alliances that last long enough to pull off major operations. You, functioning within a lawful and moral framework, can harness the same depth of strategic thinking—minus the treachery.

The Art of Trust in a Distrustful World

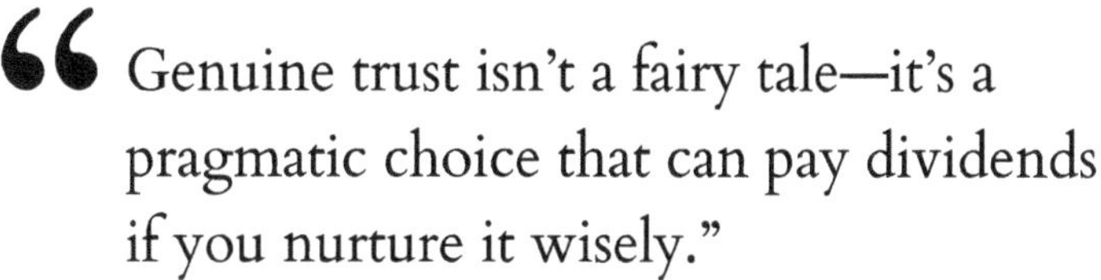

> "Genuine trust isn't a fairy tale—it's a pragmatic choice that can pay dividends if you nurture it wisely."

Every day, prosecutors and criminals share hidden understandings behind closed doors, negotiating plea deals that serve both sides. Corporate titans form joint ventures with competitors to expand into new markets, each side warily eyeing the other's bottom line. The truth is, no alliance is free from the possibility of deceit. But when trust does take root, it can accelerate breakthroughs that elude solitary endeavors.

Your objective is to approach alliances with eyes wide open, never forfeiting your moral or strategic vantage. If criminals can unite without devouring each other—and they often do—why can't legitimate powerbrokers do the same, forging networks that elevate entire industries, regions, or communities? Indeed, the difference is that ethical alliances can outlast fear-based ones, because they're constructed on a foundation of shared benefit rather than mutual blackmail.

By actively seeking collaboration, practicing open communication, and yet safeguarding critical details, you can become the linchpin that unites diverse actors under a common goal. Whether you dream of orchestrating a multinational merger or unifying a fractured local community, the blueprint of alliance-building stays consistent: grasp each side's needs, protect each side's interests, and project the kind of reliability that invites ongoing loyalty rather than fleeting convenience.

From the Pier to the Boardroom—and Beyond

> Alliances weave destinies together. Choose your partners with foresight, and your path expands exponentially."

Returning to that salt-stained pier, where a criminal power broker and a high-level attorney quietly formed a pact: the significance lies not in their moral differences but in their pragmatic alignment. Each possessed something the other lacked—a route to survival. The same logic flows through corporate halls, government negotiations, and personal relationships. You discover that where your abilities, resources, or insights end, someone else's might begin.

Building alliances is not merely a tactic. It's a philosophy that acknowledges our collective interdependence. Criminals realize they can't flourish without mules, fences, or corrupt officials. Lawyers thrive by networking with accountants, expert witnesses, or specialized colleagues. In your life, you may need advisors, mentors, or allied businesses to spark the next breakthrough.

In the upcoming chapters, we'll delve further into how these alliances function on a day-to-day level, exploring how hustlers stay under the radar and avoid drawing undue attention to their expanding sphere of influence. For now, let this truth anchor your thinking: no matter how adept your criminal cunning or how polished your legal discipline, you stand to gain immeasurably when you find the right people to stand beside you.

After all, power often grows fastest when shared wisely, forging a backbone of mutual respect. And in a world as unpredictable as ours, *knowing you can rely on others—while they rely on you—can make the difference between precarious success and unshakable dominion.*

Even the mightiest fortress needs allies—like pillars that support its walls, ensuring it remains unbreached by the storms of fortune."

11
Staying Under the Radar

> "The loudest person in the room is often the weakest."

The city's pulse quickened after midnight, a mosaic of swirling headlights and neon reflections dancing on rain-soaked streets. In the corner booth of a dimly lit café—one that stayed open to accommodate the restless and the unscrupulous alike—sat two men. Neither stood out in appearance. They wore muted jackets and nondescript caps that softened their faces in the café's subdued lighting. If you passed them by, you'd notice nothing unusual—just another late-night conversation about business or a family matter. Yet the hush in their voices and the intensity in their postures hinted at something more consequential unfolding under the cloak of dark.

Moments before, these two had finalized an agreement: a minor shipment would arrive at the docks, no questions asked, and a small but critical favor would be called in at a later date. Unlike the flamboyant crime bosses who drove flashy cars and flaunted expensive suits, these operators preferred anonymity, slipping in and out of the city's churn like phantoms. Neither sought public recognition or headlines. In their world, power thrived on obscurity, and the less others knew, the better.

This chapter, *Staying Under the Radar*, lifts the veil on how criminals and lawyers—and indeed anyone with ambition—can achieve grand aims without becoming a target. If you've ever wondered why some movers and shakers pass through chaotic upheavals unscathed, consider that they often keep to the shadows by deliberate choice. They exercise what we might call *the power of invisibility*. It's not literal magic, but a subtle synergy of low-profile habits, strategic discretion, and careful relationship management.

The Quiet Force—Why Invisibility Matters

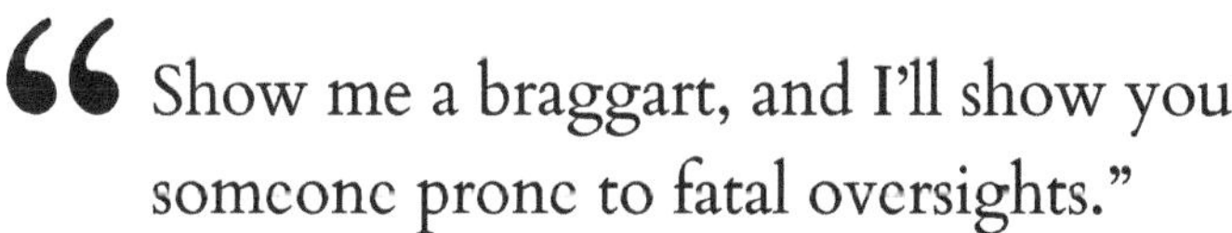

In the criminal underworld, publicity is the enemy. The moment you attract headlines, law enforcement and rivals alike close in, dissecting your every move. Even legitimate tycoons can be toppled if the media or regulatory bodies sense a scandal. In both spheres, the more conspicuous you become, the likelier you are to lose the element of surprise and invite unwanted scrutiny.

For lawyers, a wise attorney knows that flamboyance in the courtroom might sway some jurors, but it can also spur judges or opposing counsel to dig deeper. High-profile attorneys often find themselves under relentless media glare, their personal lives dissected. Meanwhile, a discreet legal strategist quietly dismantles cases by sifting through technicalities—avoiding press conferences and photo ops, emerging only when the verdict is in their favor.

In your own life—be it in business, advocacy, or personal ambitions—*staying under the radar* can grant you room to maneuver without constant second-guessing from peers, opponents, or watchers on the sidelines. It allows you to craft strategies, form alliances, and adjust course with minimal interference. You sidestep the pitfalls of inflated expectations and jealous competitors who'd love to sabotage your rise.

Discretion Over Display—Crafting a Low-Profile Aura

> Invisibility grows in the space between your accomplishments and your need for validation."

People often succumb to the urge to boast about victories—posting updates on social media, bragging about promotions, or flaunting new cars as trophies.

Criminals who manage long, successful runs know better. They might live in modest apartments or drive average vehicles, consciously avoiding the temptations of conspicuous wealth. Lawyers and corporate leaders, too, might adopt quieter lifestyles, resisting the impulse to broadcast every success or windfall.

Practical application for you:

- **Social Media Restraint:** Consider limiting what you share. Keep achievements discreet. An occasional post is fine, but constant self-promotion or flaunting can alert rivals to your patterns and resources.
- **Muted Celebrations:** When a major deal closes, celebrate quietly. For instance, treat a trusted few to a private dinner, rather than throwing a lavish party or broadcasting the news to all.
- **Humble Symbols of Success:** Drive a reliable car rather than a luxury brand that telegraphs wealth. Dress well, but avoid overtly expensive brands that can set tongues wagging.

The goal is not to forsake enjoyment but to balance it with a protective layer of *opacity*. Criminals thrive in the shadows because they're difficult to spot—and so can you, in your own version of strategic self-protection.

Strategic Camouflage—Blending with the Crowd

> "If you dress, speak, and act like everyone else, you become a ghost in plain sight."

High-level criminals will sometimes assume roles like a mild-mannered accountant, a courteous airline steward, or a traveling business consultant—archetypes that draw little interest. They master the local vernacular, keep appearances modest, and slip into day-to-day routines that raise no eyebrows. Even in the corporate or social sphere, adopting a neutral presentation can help you slide under radars.

Consider a real-world scenario: a tech entrepreneur might skip the flashy Silicon Valley uniform of hoodies and limousines, instead blending with local professionals in business-casual attire. They attend conferences quietly, ask astute questions without hogging the microphone. Their presence registers as polite yet unremarkable. Behind the scenes, however, they may be forging a groundbreaking merger or stealthily recruiting top talent.

In the realm of law, a defense attorney who avoids theatrical courtroom tactics can lull the prosecution into underestimating their case. They project calm rationality, letting the opposition believe there's little fight to be had—then strike hard with carefully timed evidence. The principle remains: to *fade into the background* so thoroughly that opponents never suspect the magnitude of the storm brewing beneath your calm exterior.

Cultivating Sentries—Eyes on the Periphery

In shadows, it pays to have watchers who can warn you of the light."

Criminal organizations maintain networks of informants—restaurant staff, taxi drivers, or low-level operators who monitor the streets for police presence or rival threats. This allows them to stay one step ahead, shifting locations or altering plans in a heartbeat. Similarly, successful professionals—CEOs, politicians, or influential lawyers—surround themselves with vigilant assistants, analysts, and allies who feed them intel on emerging hazards or opportunities.

For you, consider building a circle of trusted associates who help you track industry trends, competitor moves, or even social undercurrents that could affect your projects. You don't need to adopt a cloak-and-dagger approach, but a network of reliable "eyes on the ground" ensures you're not blindsided. It might be a friend in a rival firm, an industry insider who's willing to share tips informally, or a well-connected mentor who keeps tabs on shifting market tides.

Be sure to reciprocate value—keep your watchers informed of developments that might interest them. Criminals reward informants with small cuts of profits; legitimate players offer reciprocal support, advice, or referrals. Over time, you'll develop a network that quietly extends your reach, allowing you to remain unseen yet deeply informed.

Operational Security—Guarding Your Digital Footprint

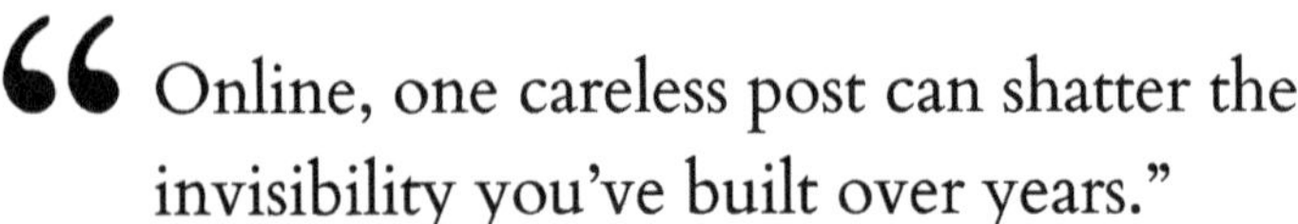

> “Online, one careless post can shatter the invisibility you’ve built over years.”

In the modern world, secrecy isn’t just about physical presence—it’s about data trails. Criminals who excel at evading capture often use encrypted messaging apps, adopt multiple devices under aliases, and avoid location tagging. On the flip side, legitimate professionals who value discretion keep personal lives off LinkedIn and Instagram, maintaining separate communication channels for business vs. private matters.

Consider these digital hygiene steps:

- **Segregate Communications:** Use distinct emails for different ventures. If you’re running multiple projects, keep them compartmentalized so a breach in one domain doesn’t expose the rest.
- **Limit Metadata:** Disable location services on photos or chat apps. Refrain from checking into public venues in real time.
- **Watch Privacy Settings:** Regularly review the privacy defaults on social platforms. Many sites update terms frequently, loosening user protections without explicit notice.

While you needn’t adopt a criminal’s paranoia, a healthy vigilance can spare you from data leaks that sabotage business plans or personal aspirations. Simple oversights—like sharing flight details publicly—can tip off potential adversaries to your travel schedule, leaving you vulnerable.

Silence as a Weapon—Underplaying Your Intent

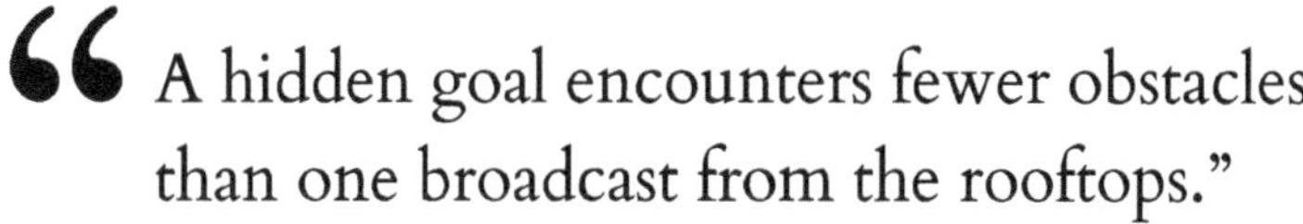

In high-stakes circles, the less people know about your target, the less they can obstruct you. Criminals mask their ultimate plans—mules believe they’re only shipping harmless goods, or crew members see just a sliver of the whole heist. By fragmenting knowledge, criminals ensure no single defector can unravel everything.

For legitimate entrepreneurs or lawyers, a parallel tactic is to keep specifics of major deals under wraps until the final hour. A corporate acquisition, for instance, could be quietly in the works for months before a public announcement. The advantage? Competitors don’t have time to sabotage the deal or swoop in with a counter-offer. Lawyers often counsel clients to remain tight-lipped about lawsuit strategies, revealing critical evidence only when timing grants maximal leverage.

In day-to-day life, silence can be your shield. If you have an ambitious plan—be it a job change, an investment, or a project pivot—consider who truly needs to know. Over-sharing can invite envy or sabotage from those who feel threatened by your forward momentum.

Instead, let your actions speak. By the time you unveil your accomplishment, your foundation is already secure.

The Art of Deflection and Misdirection

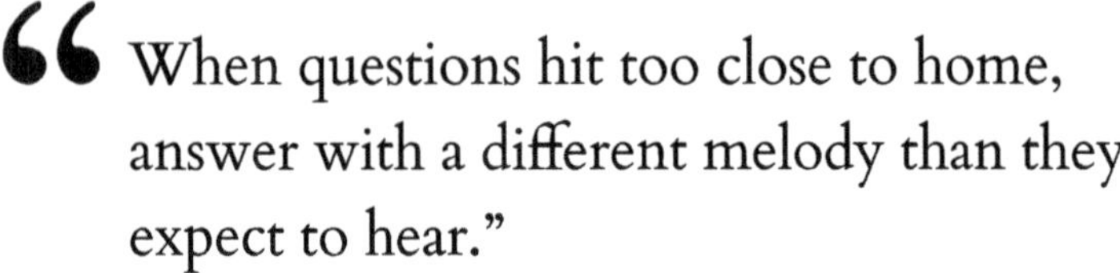

> "When questions hit too close to home, answer with a different melody than they expect to hear."

Criminals caught in a sudden spotlight often deflect suspicion by offering partial truths or feigned vulnerabilities. Perhaps they spin a sob story of financial hardship, drawing pity instead of scrutiny. Or they drop an irrelevant detail that leads nosy investigators down a false trail. Either way, they redirect prying eyes away from the hidden reality.

For professionals, this skill can manifest more benignly. If a colleague asks probing questions about a confidential project, you might respond with broad strokes: "It's still in exploratory stages, just analyzing options." You provide enough of a reply to satisfy curiosity without divulging crucial details. Or if rumors circulate about your next career move, you can drop ambiguous hints that you're "weighing various paths," effectively changing the subject and maintaining an aura of unpredictability.

Deflection doesn't imply dishonesty; it's about protecting sensitive information. Not every query deserves a full disclosure. By steering conversations toward safer topics, you minimize risk and control your narrative.

The Imperative of Emotional Control

> "Rage, pride, or panic will paint a bull's-eye on your back—stay calm, stay invisible."

One of the most common ways people blow their low profile is through emotional outbursts. A criminal who loudly threatens a rival or humiliates a subordinate in public signals vulnerability. Similarly, a lawyer who lets frustration show in court reveals possible weaknesses that opposing counsel can exploit.

Emotional discipline is key to staying under the radar. If someone attacks your ideas or undermines your progress, responding with explosive anger only escalates attention. Instead, adopt a cool, measured tone. Let them glimpse neither your fury nor your fear. By maintaining composure, you telegraph quiet confidence. People often lose interest in provoking someone who refuses to be provoked.

In practical terms, this means cultivating a mental "pause button." Before snapping back at a provocation, take a breath, formulate a level-headed response, and deliver it in a calm, almost neutral manner. Watch as the aggressor struggles to stir you. Meanwhile, onlookers see a professional, unflappable demeanor—a hallmark of someone not to be trifled with.

Keeping Networks Muted Yet Active

> "In the game of shadows, a whisper can achieve more than a public rallying cry."

Consider how criminals coordinate operations. They rarely hold giant gatherings. Instead, they use tight circles and coded communication, ensuring each participant knows just enough to fulfill their role. Legitimate power networks can emulate this discreet model. Instead of a high-profile conference with media coverage, you might host small, off-the-record think tanks. Instead of mass emails, use direct calls or quietly arranged meetups to discuss pivotal moves.

By maintaining these muted methods, you keep your network functioning without broadcasting every initiative to rivals. The result: you can forge alliances, share resources, or launch joint ventures with minimal fanfare, depriving outside forces of time to mount a counter-strategy.

An added benefit: your collaborators feel a sense of exclusivity. When they recognize they're part of a select inner circle, loyalty tends to solidify. It's the psychological effect criminals harness when they designate specific crew members as "trusted lieutenants." In a legitimate context, it strengthens your network's cohesion while preserving your ability to adjust or pivot under the cover of low visibility.

Accepting Praise Without Flaunting It

> Let praise find you quietly; accolades are sweetest when they arrive unbidden."

One reason stealthy players remain under the radar is they don't actively chase public accolades. When recognition comes—maybe a promotion, an industry award, or a successful legal win—they accept it modestly, often redirecting credit to team members or mentors. This approach further dims the spotlight on them personally.

A criminal boss who publicly boasts about every score draws law enforcement like moths to a flame. Similarly, a lawyer who constantly self-promotes in legal journals might attract envious colleagues or extra scrutiny from bar associations. By contrast, the operator who maintains a low-key presence can slip from victory to victory with less friction.

So when success does kiss your doorstep, see if you can channel the spotlight into a broader narrative—praise the collaborative effort, the supportive environment, or sheer luck. This diminishes jealousy and positions you as a team player rather than a showboat. Your peers notice you're not scrambling for the limelight, which ironically can earn you deeper respect and trust.

Standing Out Only When Necessary

> "Invisibility isn't a vow of perpetual silence; it's knowing when to speak so that every word lands like a hammer."

The fact you choose to remain under the radar most of the time doesn't mean you must never assert yourself. Criminals occasionally make calculated displays of power—unmistakable warnings that they're not to be crossed. Lawyers may reserve theatrical courtroom flourishes for the moments that genuinely sway a jury.

You, too, can cultivate a sense of timing. If you consistently operate in a subdued manner, then decide one day to deliver a bold presentation or take a firm stand on an issue, it commands heightened attention. People think: "They rarely push forward this strongly; it must be critical." Your voice gains gravity precisely because you don't overuse it.

This tactic works in any setting. If you're known for seldom speaking up in meetings, the day you raise your hand with a compelling viewpoint, colleagues will listen. If you typically avoid public debates, the instance you step onto a stage, the audience leans in, expecting something substantial. By limiting your overt displays, you preserve the element of surprise, turning your occasional spotlight moments into potent leverage points.

The Ethical Underpinning of Stealth

> "Avoiding attention doesn't mean hiding wrongdoing; sometimes it's the path to ensure your good deeds aren't derailed by envy or interference."

In the criminal realm, stealth is about evading justice. But for law-abiding individuals, *staying under the radar* serves an entirely different purpose—protection from malicious competitors, trolls, or unwarranted intrusions. You may simply want to develop innovative ideas without external sabotage or build a financial cushion without attracting opportunists.

Being discreet isn't about deception or unethical secrecy; it's about **focus**—the capacity to work diligently without the noise of constant scrutiny. By selectively revealing your pursuits, you ward off those who might meddle out of jealousy, prejudice, or vested interest. You also avoid making promises prematurely, thus shielding your reputation from the disappointment of goals that don't materialize.

Ultimately, the moral litmus test for "staying under the radar" lies in *intent.* If your aim is to circumvent accountability for unethical acts, stealth morphs into something sinister. But if your goal is to safeguard a vision until it's robust enough to withstand external forces, you're simply practicing prudent self-preservation.

The Nexus of Cunning and Lawful Prudence

> “Let the criminals scurry in darkness to evade their crimes; let the wise tread softly to protect their brilliance.”

One might ask: *What can we legitimately learn from those who break the law?* The answer is: *their mastery of quiet maneuvering.* They might use it to evade justice, but the core principles—discretion, strategic camouflage, controlling emotional displays—are ethically neutral. Lawyers, corporate leaders, public servants, and everyday professionals all benefit from these principles when applying them to legitimate endeavors.

Thus, the synergy is clear: think like a criminal in terms of avoiding spotlight vulnerabilities, but act like a lawyer by remaining grounded in legality and ethics. A stealthy approach combined with a solid moral compass grants you a formidable edge—people rarely see your moves coming, but when they do, they find nothing blameworthy to latch onto.

From Shadows to Subtle Success

> “A seed germinates beneath the soil—unseen yet unyielding—until it’s ready to break through in full bloom.”

For those charting ambitious life paths—be it launching a startup, expanding an existing venture, or simply fortifying a personal goal—*under-the-radar tactics* serve as both shield and sword. When you operate quietly, you're free from the stress of constant external opinion. You can pivot swiftly without making headlines. You can forge alliances behind closed doors, test prototypes privately, or refine your craft to perfection.

When your work finally emerges, it does so with a momentum that catches onlookers off guard. Suddenly, they see the results: a product launch, a legal victory, a striking work of art—and they wonder, "Where did this come from?" Meanwhile, you've sidestepped the endless friction of public scrutiny or sabotage.

In the chapters to come, we'll transition to the *Ethics of Power*—exploring how to tread the line between harnessing these potent strategies and succumbing to the temptations that corrupt. For now, remember that in a world clamoring for attention, sometimes the brightest triumph belongs to those who master the art of invisibility. The loudest person in the room might hog the spotlight, but as every hustler, lawyer, and strategic visionary knows, true power often belongs to the silent architect working behind the scenes.

So take this lesson, weave it into your professional and personal tapestry: *Stay quiet, move wisely, and let your actions speak only when you're ready for the world to listen.*

“The shadows are not merely a place to hide—they are the workshop where the unspoken genius of your plan quietly forges victory.”

PART IV

The Ethics of Power

12

Walking the Fine Line

> “Power corrupts, but wisdom keeps it in check.”

The penthouse suite of the Grand Concordia Hotel sprawled across the entire top floor, its panoramic windows revealing a city glittering like a promise in the night. Within the hushed confines of that lofty space, two figures stood by the floor-to-ceiling glass, silhouettes against a backdrop of endless neon. One wore the poised demeanor of a seasoned defense attorney—tailored suit immaculate, hair meticulously brushed, an undeniable air of authority in every measured gesture. The other carried a more restless energy, someone accustomed to sidestepping rules and dancing in the gray. Their body language hinted at a tension neither dared to fully expose.

Outside, the skyscraper spires and pulsing roads testified to humanity's undying ambition. But here, in the penthouse's softly lit interior, the talk was not of expansion or grandiose deals—*it was of boundaries.* A lucrative scheme lay on the table. In purely strategic terms, it was brilliant: a framework of shell companies, falsified contracts, and well-placed legal loopholes that could funnel untold profits to the parties involved. Yet a question hung heavy in the air: *How far will we go before we lose ourselves?*

That question—so faint yet so persistent—echoes throughout this chapter. For we have journeyed deep into the dual mindset of *criminal cunning* and *legal discipline*, gleaning the potent advantages of seeing through illusions, reading the unspoken codes of power, and employing stealthy maneuvers that shield us from prying eyes. We have witnessed how these tools, fused, can yield near-invincible strategies. But we now arrive at a moral and spiritual crossroads: **Walking the Fine Line** means learning where to halt, lest these formidable methods ensnare us in a labyrinth of our own making.

> "There is a point at which cunning transforms into deceit, and discipline mutates into corruption. The question is: can you sense that point before it's too late?"

In the penthouse, the restless figure turned, eyes flicking toward the attorney. A hush enveloped them, broken only by the faint hum of the city below. Perhaps the tension came from guilt—a whisper of conscience that insisted they understand the stakes. Or maybe it was the quiet fear that once you cross certain boundaries, no apology or justification can undo the damage. The attorney, lips pressed together in a carefully neutral line, said nothing. Yet in the reflection of that glass wall, both saw their own doubts.

Such doubts rarely erupt in a dramatic swirl at first. More often, they creep into your peripheral vision, disguised as *minor compromises*. You rationalize them: you are simply using the system's weaknesses, or you are bending rules that you believe stifle genuine progress. You say to yourself, *just this once*, or *everyone else is doing it, so why not me?* With each step, the line between *necessary cunning* and *harmful deceit* recedes into the distance.

Those who claim that criminals operate without a moral compass are mistaken. Even in the underworld, unspoken codes of honor exist. Yet just as easily, those codes can be twisted to justify cruelty or betrayal. Likewise, in the ivory corridors of legal practice, some lawyers succumb to the allure of winning at any cost, discarding the deeper purpose behind laws and justice. *The difference is not that criminals have no conscience and lawyers do; it is that both wrestle with the temptation to sacrifice what is right for what is profitable.*

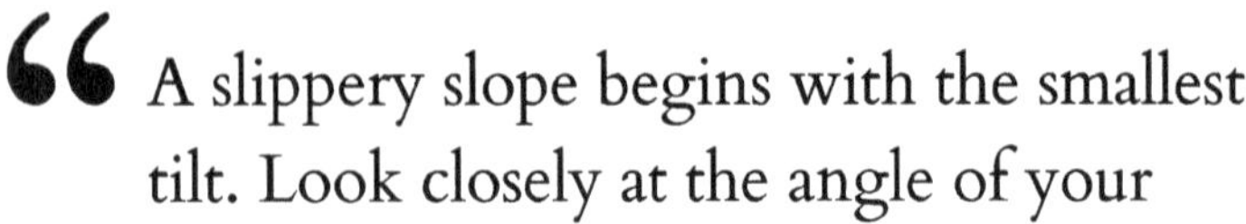
“ A slippery slope begins with the smallest tilt. Look closely at the angle of your

intent, and you might save yourself from a catastrophic plunge."

That slope can appear in countless forms. A paralegal at a prestigious firm might decide to hide a piece of exculpatory evidence because the client paying the bills is too influential to offend. A small-time con artist might rationalize that forging a signature to release funds from a dormant account harms no one. A district attorney, desperate for a high-profile conviction, could be tempted to exaggerate evidence or pressure a reluctant witness. Each scenario depicts the same moral tension: the desire for an outcome that overshadows the quiet voice that asks, *What cost will be paid?*

In times of triumph, that voice can be drowned out by applause, accolades, or the allure of quick money. But eventually, the hollow ring of unscrupulous victory can gnaw at one's psyche. Those who lose themselves to corruption rarely do so overnight. More often, they slip into it like an actor slipping further into character until they can no longer separate the performance from reality.

A well-placed lawyer can rationalize anything: a 'necessary evil,' a minor bending of the statute. A cunning hustler can justify an illusion, calling it business as usual. But when does that justification break faith with your soul?"

Consider the figure in the penthouse who never intended to cross lines. Perhaps they began with admirable motives: providing for their family, proving their worth in a cutthroat environment, or simply craving a life free from subjugation. Over time, they realized that truly scaling the heights of influence demanded unorthodox methods. They learned to read people as a predator does, to see vulnerabilities and micro-expressions, to manipulate negotiations with lethal precision. Then they discovered how lawyers, with their mastery of statutes and precedents, could construct fortresses around morally dubious actions.

At first, it felt almost exhilarating. The system that once oppressed them now seemed pliable under their skilled hands. But in the reflection of the penthouse window, they might see a glimpse of who they used to be—someone who believed in fairness, or at least in certain lines that shouldn't be crossed. And across from them, the attorney, presumably a paragon of law, wonders whether their professional code is morphing into a tapestry of convenient interpretations that betray the essence of justice.

Such moments of self-awareness can be chilling, for they illuminate just how easy it is to drift from cunning into an ethical wasteland. Yet self-awareness also births the chance for redemption: *the opportunity to reevaluate, to realign with principles that keep one's humanity intact.* Indeed, many who rise to the brink of moral compromise find renewed purpose in stepping back, reasserting boundaries, and forging alliances with like-minded souls who value long-term integrity over transient gains.

> “True power, it turns out, does not rest solely on manipulation or legal subterfuge. It thrives when you build it upon unwavering principles that, paradoxically, make your cunning even more effective.”

Why? Because trust, even in the underworld, remains the ultimate currency. Everyone wants to align with an operator who, for all their slyness, still respects certain lines of loyalty and fairness. Criminals who betray partners at every turn find themselves perpetually on the run; attorneys who lie outright to judges or clients face devastating professional censure. Though we often think of these realms—crime and law—as polar opposites, both revolve around *confidence* and *credibility*. A contract, whether illegal or legal, hinges on the belief that terms will be honored. Once that belief shatters, alliances crumble.

The wise learn to cultivate a reputation that, while benefiting from cunning and legal dexterity, upholds a code of conduct. They might be secretive, but they do not betray every vow. They might manipulate negotiations, but they do not sabotage the innocent. Their moral code might not conform to polite society’s standards in every respect, yet they remain loyal to a personal ethos that stops them from spiraling into total moral oblivion.

Walking the Fine Line thus extends beyond mere legal compliance. It is an act of self-preservation for both your spirit and your societal standing. The criminal who refuses to harm children, for instance, or the lawyer who refuses to fabricate evidence despite immense pressure, both exhibit the principle that cunning need not equal cruelty, and discipline need not devolve into moral compromise. These boundaries, though fluid, offer a form of self-respect that transcends monetary or reputational gains.

In that lofty penthouse suite, the conversation might continue late into the night. Plans would be dissected, potential fallout assessed. The participants would weigh whether to pull back or to press on with a scheme that skirts legality and threatens their moral bearings. Each would have to decide how far they are willing to push *the synergy of cunning and law* before it becomes a poison in their veins. If they choose to proceed heedlessly, they embark on a path that could bring short-term success but also sow seeds of betrayal, guilt, or eventual downfall. If they choose caution and decency, they might forfeit immediate gains yet discover a different breed of power—one that cannot be so easily toppled by scandal or shame.

> “Ultimately, the line you walk is drawn in the silence of your own conscience. If you can cross it without remorse, you will find only hollow victory. If you can uphold it, you may find a deeper sense of authority—over yourself and your destiny—than any cunning ploy can grant.”

Such is the delicate balance between criminal insight and legal acumen. You can glean from the criminal mind a remarkable alertness to human flaws, an ability to read the hidden textures of power, and a fearless drive to seize opportunities. From the lawyer's discipline, you harness structured knowledge of rules, ethical codes, and advocacy that shields you from reckless missteps. And from your own moral intuition, you glean the wisdom to know when enough is enough—to understand that real success shines brightest when not stained by needless harm or duplicity.

When all is said and done, the echoes of that late-night conversation in the penthouse remain as a warning and a beacon. A warning, because the lure of ultimate control can seduce even the most grounded person into illusions of untouchability. A beacon, because in the choice to walk away from destructive cunning or to moderate it with ethical discipline, one shapes a destiny steeped in authenticity and respect. That is where *true power* abides—*not* in how thoroughly you can manipulate the game, but in whether you remain in command of your integrity as you do so.

Power corrupts, but wisdom keeps it in check. You stand now at the threshold: step carefully, for the line between brilliance and self-betrayal can be thinner than a whisper."

13

The Consequences of Power

> "Power, once unleashed without conscience, carves paths that can lead to triumph—or ruin."

A hush settled over the grand marble foyer of an opulent estate that sprawled across acres of prime countryside. Under a glittering chandelier, guests in designer gowns and sleek tuxedos glided around with champagne flutes, feigning effortless grace. The host—a flamboyant tycoon famed for his razor-sharp mind and rumored criminal ties—stood at the top of a sweeping staircase, watching over the gathering like a monarch surveying a kingdom. There was a time, not too long ago, when he was a mere whisper in the corridors of influence—no one recognized his face or name. Yet here he stood now, commanding attention, his fortunes built on a potent blend of *criminal cunning* and *legal discipline.*

At a glance, the scene resembled a glamorous celebration of success: shimmering laughter, polite clinks of glass, men and women trying to outdo each other in silent competition. But if you looked closer, you might discern small cracks in the composure. Anxious eyes darted toward the staircase, as though expecting an announcement that might redefine alliances or topple reputations. In the corner, a stern-faced attorney spoke quietly with two edgy investors, both of whom had poured wealth into the tycoon's ventures, half-suspecting the foundation beneath them might be rotten. Somewhere above, behind locked doors, incriminating paperwork lay carefully hidden—insurance against betrayal.

That night, the tycoon's empire loomed like a fortress. Yet in a matter of weeks, federal investigators would storm the estate, prying into every shadowed corner. The grand foyer, once filled with cordial guests, would become eerily silent, the harpsichord replaced by the echo of footfalls on cold marble floors. His *unchecked power*, which had soared so high, would come crashing down in a spectacular scandal. And all that would remain was the cautionary tale of a brilliant operator who, blinded by ambition, ignored the cracks in his own moral foundation until it collapsed beneath him.

It is that *collapse*—the harsh consequences faced by those who fail to heed the warnings inherent in power—that forms the core of this chapter. Since the earliest pages of this book, we have explored how merging the raw instincts of a criminal with the disciplined knowledge of law can catapult you to remarkable heights. *Yet there is a limit to how far cunning can stretch before it backfires.* Time and again, history recounts individuals who soared too close to the sun on wings stitched together by half-truths, brazen manipulations, or ruthless exploitation, only to be undone by the same forces they had once mastered.

> “Power, once unleashed without conscience, carves paths that can lead to triumph—or ruin. A cunning mind sees the path, but a wise mind also sees the chasm at its edge.”

The annals of business, politics, and crime are littered with such downfalls. Mafia bosses who believed their brutal tactics made them untouchable found themselves betrayed by underlings or cornered by federal racketeering charges. Corporate moguls, having massaged numbers in a labyrinth of fraudulent transactions, collapsed under the weight of unstoppable audits, their reputations shattered and fortunes stripped. Influential politicians, once shielded by loyal sycophants, crumbled at the first sign of a media expose that revealed hush money or concealed bribes. No matter how ingenious the scheme, the dual threat of *law* and *public scrutiny* can turn a fortress into a tomb in the blink of an eye.

Moreover, the consequences of power misused do not merely ruin careers or finances—they strike at the very foundation of relationships and personal identity.

The criminal mastermind who once commanded loyalty through intimidation can find that loyalty dissolves like dust when adversity strikes, leaving him isolated. The brilliant attorney who twisted the law to secure unjust victories might see her professional peers ostracize her, her license threatened, her sense of self-worth corroded by the knowledge that the justice she once served has become her victim. *In the end, the intangible loss—a sense of dignity, trust, or belonging—can cut deeper than any prison sentence or headline scandal.*

This is not to say that power must inherently corrupt. Rather, *unrestrained* power, guided solely by ambition, can distort perspectives until you no longer sense the lines you are crossing. A hustler who soared by leveraging every advantage might begin rationalizing unethical choices as mere "business tactics." A lawyer, in pursuit of winning, could slip from strategic omissions to outright fabrication. Neither sets out to become the villain; each simply feeds the beast of expediency until it grows too large to contain.

> Power can be a miracle if wielded justly, or a monster if fed with disregard for consequence. The line between the two is thinner than most dare to admit."

There are vivid real-life stories of those who tumbled from seemingly unassailable heights. One can think of the fall of Bernard Madoff, who constructed a glittering Ponzi empire that dazzled even the most sophisticated investors—until the day his entire scheme collapsed like a house of cards. Or the downfall of a once-respected district attorney who tampered with evidence in the name of "public safety," only to watch every case he ever touched get called into question. Or those corporate titans who soared on cooked books, their stocks inflating to unsustainable levels, before the inevitable unraveling left thousands jobless.

In each of these stories, *the final price was not just legal trouble*, though fines and prison terms often ensued. There was also the harrowing sense of betrayal—both of others and of themselves. Family members left in ruin, friends distancing themselves to protect their own reputations, and a public that gleefully turned them into cautionary headlines. The illusions of invincibility or brilliance dissolved instantly, replaced by the stark reality that *no one is beyond the reach of accountability*.

And so, how do we avoid such pitfalls? How do we maintain a vantage that grants us cunning—sharp awareness of opportunities and vulnerabilities—without poisoning our moral center?

The answer lies in balancing the thirst for advantage with an unflinching awareness of potential repercussions. It calls us to remain anchored in the same *legal discipline* we use to protect ourselves from reckless risk, but to extend that discipline into an ethical realm. The truly powerful individual, the one who endures beyond the ephemeral limelight, is the one who *knows where to draw the line*. They refuse to treat loyalty as a disposable asset, they consider the broader social and personal impact of their maneuvers, and they recognize that no empire is worth building if it stands on the graves of those they betrayed or abused.

> “True power is not a short-lived blaze of glory; it's a sustainable flame that warms your path without scorching everything around you.”

Reflect, too, on the nature of alliances. Building them, as explored in earlier chapters, can elevate you to new heights. But alliances formed under deceit or fear soon unravel. Those anchored in mutual respect and transparent benefit stand resilient through storms. The con artist who coerces loyalty with threats reaps only a fleeting advantage, while the strategic leader who fosters genuine goodwill amasses a robust network that can outlast any crisis.

For lawyers, the *rules of professional conduct* exist not merely to stifle creativity but to ensure that the profession retains public trust. Abusing the system through endless loopholes or encouraging clients to act in ways that blatantly violate the spirit of the law inevitably leads to professional censure or disbarment. The immediate payoff of winning a high-profile case through questionable means pales in comparison to the long-term respect and continuity that come from upholding the core values of justice.

Criminal cunning can highlight shortcuts or reveal unguarded weaknesses in systems. But the moment that cunning is fueled purely by greed or the desire to control, the user becomes ensnared in a trap of endless escalation. They must lie bigger next time, conceal more evidence, or intimidate more witnesses just to maintain the façade. And with each escalation, the blowback grows exponentially. Like a gambler doubling down on each bet, eventually the resources—be they money, credibility, or loyal allies—run dry, and the final wager consumes everything.

> “When you stand at a precipice and see an opportunity that demands you compromise your integrity, remember that a short leap can plunge you into an abyss from which return is almost impossible.”

One might wonder: *Is it then safer to shun power altogether?* The answer is not that we should fear or reject power, but that we must cultivate an internal governor that checks its extremes. Ambition is not evil in itself. Neither is wanting to outmaneuver rivals or secure a formidable position. The key is maintaining an unwavering connection to the consequences. For each action, trace the potential ripple effects—who stands to be harmed, what trust may be broken, what irreparable mark might you leave on your own conscience.

It is also vital to remember that the line between cunning and corruption becomes thinner under stress or success. During times of crisis, desperation can drive once-honest people to make dire mistakes. And at the apex of success, arrogance can tempt them to believe they are untouchable. Surviving these extremes demands grounding—whether through personal ethics, a circle of trusted advisers who speak truth unfiltered, or a mindful humility that understands no fortress is unbreachable.

And so we arrive at the caution and the hope of this chapter. **The Consequences of Power** need not be fatal if we hold ourselves accountable. If you can blend the mindful cunning of a criminal, the protective discipline of a lawyer, and the moral clarity of a balanced soul, you stand a chance of wielding power that enhances rather than destroys. You can, in other words, cultivate a formidable presence that thrives on knowledge instead of exploitation, on alliances rather than subjugation, and on strategic brilliance that coexists with basic human decency.

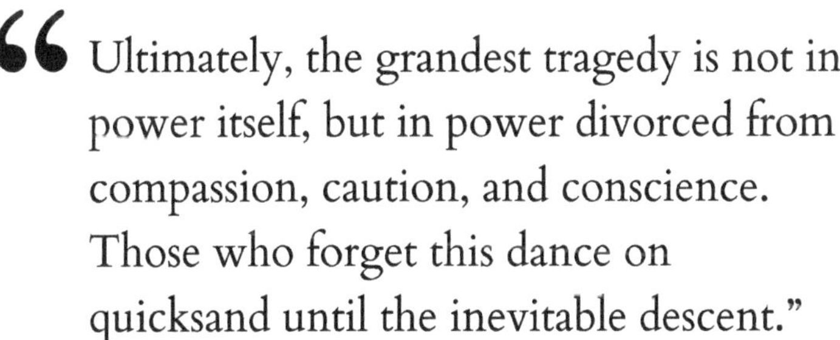

> "Ultimately, the grandest tragedy is not in power itself, but in power divorced from compassion, caution, and conscience. Those who forget this dance on quicksand until the inevitable descent."

Within the story of the gilded penthouse and the flamboyant tycoon, there is a lesson etched in gold: those who fail to heed that lesson end up as cautionary tales whispered about over quiet dinners, their names invoked as reminders that no empire is truly invincible. The price of ignoring consequences is high. Yet the reward for respecting them is a power that can endure, a legacy that outlasts the fleeting illusions conjured by pure cunning.

And that is where your journey stands now—on the brink of new decisions and fresh ambitions. Will you proceed blindly, amassing secrets and deceptions until they bury you? Or will you walk forward with an alert mind and a guarded heart, forging achievements that reflect not just brilliance but also a measure of kindness, integrity, and respect for the boundaries that protect us all from chaos?

Heed the past, weigh each step, and let your power shine untainted by the darkness that claims those who forget the final reckoning. For in the end, consequence always has the last word."

14
The Legacy of a Strategist

> "Think boldly, act wisely, and leave a legacy that speaks for itself."

A hush enveloped the banquet hall as the crowd turned its collective gaze to a solitary figure at the front of the room. Standing behind an ornate lectern carved with the regal symbols of a bygone era, that figure—a once-anonymous thinker who had orchestrated countless alliances, circumnavigated countless pitfalls, and outsmarted enemies hidden in plain sight—now looked out across a sea of faces. On this night, they were to receive a prestigious lifetime achievement award, a testament to a career forged by blending *criminal cunning* with *legal discipline* and an unwavering moral backbone.

But even in that moment of apparent triumph, a certain tension vibrated beneath the applause and bright lights. The strategist's eyes glistened with a knowledge that these accolades, while gratifying, only told a fraction of the story. Countless invisible strands held this triumph together: the uncredited confidants who had quietly shaped deals, the close calls that could have derailed everything, the internal struggles that haunted each major decision. The award could never capture the complexity of walking the razor-thin line between ambition and self-restraint. As the applause swelled, the strategist offered a faint, reflective smile, aware that the true measure of a legacy is often found not in trophies, but in the memories and transformations left behind in others.

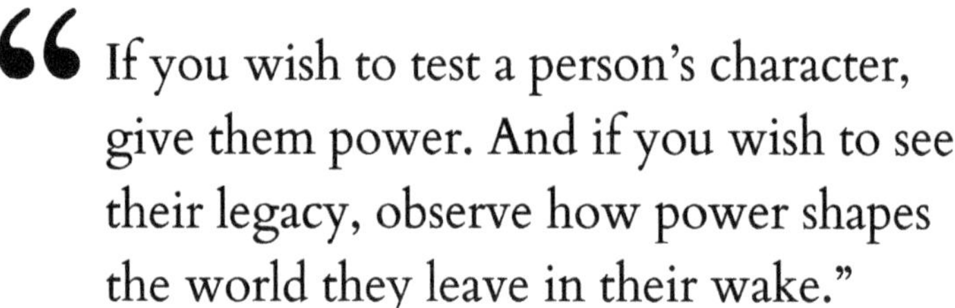

In the chapters preceding this one, we have dissected the art of cunning, the discipline of legality, the fragile ethics of power, and the subtle dance between shadowy gambits and lawful frameworks. We have seen how criminals thrive on raw opportunism—taking advantage of every oversight or vulnerability—while lawyers harness legal intricacies and procedural safeguards to fortify their moves. At the nexus of these worlds is a strategy so potent that it can unlock achievements unimaginable to those who limit themselves to conventional thinking or untempered cunning alone. Yet to ascend to the pinnacle of influence and remain unscathed, the strategist must master more than mere tactics. They must cultivate a *legacy*.

Legacies are less about personal gain and more about the imprint one's actions leave on others: the trust forged or broken, the standards upheld or compromised, the sense of possibility expanded or dashed. A criminal mind might see legacy as irrelevant—why worry about tomorrow when you thrive today? A purely legal mind might define legacy by the impact of precedents set, the case law changed, or the institutions reformed. But the most enduring strategist merges these perspectives, crafting accomplishments that outlast immediate victories and resonate through communities, businesses, or entire industries.

A master strategist looks beyond the next move and envisions the entire endgame—then shapes the board so that others may carry forth the win even after their own piece is removed."

Consider the life of a quietly brilliant negotiator who spent decades brokering deals among fierce corporate rivals. While they remained largely unknown to the public, each handshake they orchestrated built new bridges, revitalized stagnant industries, and spurred innovation in markets once stifled by hostile competition. Over time, those alliances evolved into stable frameworks that outlasted fleeting management trends and even outlasted the negotiator's own tenure. When they finally departed the scene, the business world they left behind bore the indelible mark of their strategic imprint—an enduring testament to the *legacy* they created.

In a contrasting example, one might recall a cunning attorney who devoted years to defending causes that initially raised eyebrows: whistleblowers exposing rampant corruption, marginalized communities unable to secure justice through conventional means, even reformed criminals seeking to start anew. This attorney, harnessing both the predatory instincts to see hidden weaknesses in a system and the ethical conviction to channel those insights into lawful avenues, systematically reshaped public expectations of what legal defense could accomplish. Long after that attorney set down their final case, the reverberations of their advocacy lived on in legislation, societal attitudes, and the personal stories of those lives they touched. Their legacy thrived in the hearts and minds of people they never even met—modern-day beneficiaries of the frameworks they helped establish.

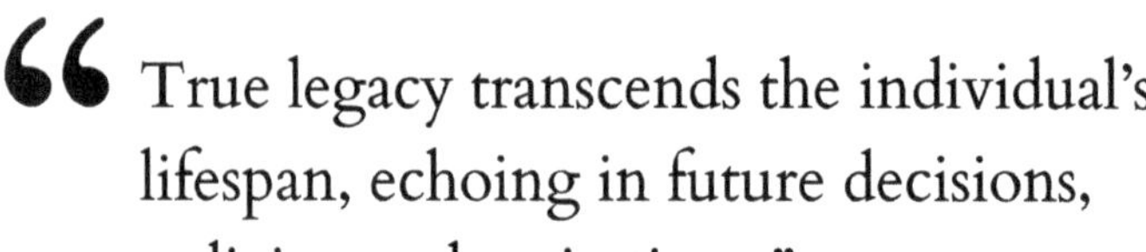

> "True legacy transcends the individual's lifespan, echoing in future decisions, policies, and aspirations."

Yet forging such a legacy demands more than mere brilliance. It requires a delicate interplay of your cunning instincts and your moral compass. Criminal acumen might tempt you to chase immediate advantage, but if you devastate too many alliances or betray too many confidences, your foundation will eventually crumble.

Legal discipline might tether you to rules, but if you never dare to think beyond conventional boundaries, you might never make a transformative impact. The strategist who endures is the one who can juggle these forces—*unleashing bold maneuvers while preserving an ethical anchor.*

Some question whether a legacy built by cunning can be morally sound. The answer lies in intent. If your cunning serves only your ego or greed, your victories will inevitably ring hollow. If, however, you employ cunning to navigate the labyrinth of complex stakeholders—balancing your interests with broader social or human considerations—your successes can foster the kind of respect that outlives you. This approach does not require sainthood. It merely demands that you remain mindful of consequences, seeking avenues of advancement that do not rely on oppression or degradation.

Every door you force open with cunning eventually requires you to show your face inside the room. If you have forgotten your ethics on the threshold, the people you meet there will remember it—and so will history."

Moreover, those who craft a lasting legacy acknowledge that *mentorship* can amplify their impact exponentially. In the criminal underworld, protégés often replicate the brutal methods of their mentors unless they find reason to evolve. Conversely, in the realm of law and high-stakes strategy, a disciple who sees not just your cunning but also your restraint becomes an ambassador of your legacy, perpetuating your ideals in future generations of leadership or negotiation. By guiding emerging talents—sharing not just tactics but also the underlying values that keep ambition from running amok—you ensure that your imprint is not merely personal but generational.

There is also a paradox to reckon with: sometimes, the greatest legacy is shaped by acts that are invisible to the public eye. You might orchestrate a crucial détente between warring factions, remain a silent investor in philanthropic ventures, or quietly counsel an up-and-coming leader to avoid pitfalls that nearly destroyed you. These achievements may never garnish front-page coverage or social media adulation, but they can alter the trajectories of entire lives or institutions. Such quiet influence resonates longer than sensational headlines, precisely because it rests on genuine commitment rather than ephemeral publicity.

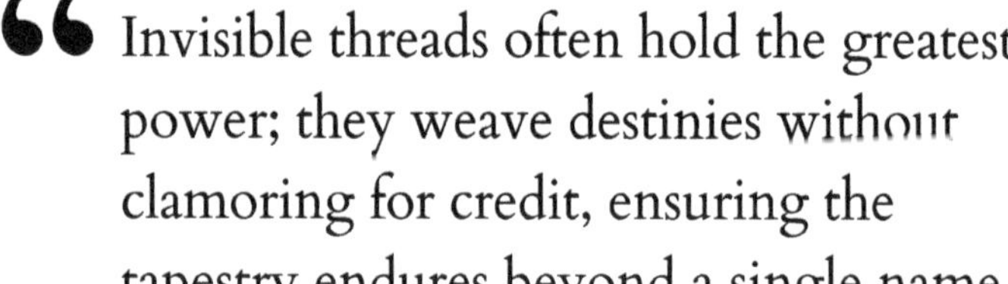

> “Invisible threads often hold the greatest power; they weave destinies without clamoring for credit, ensuring the tapestry endures beyond a single name or face.”

Legacy also bears an emotional dimension. The strategist who commands respect in a boardroom but leaves behind shattered familial bonds reaps only a partial success. True legacy weaves through the fabric of personal relationships as well—friends, partners, children. Power that tramples these domains leaves behind bitterness, a void that wealth or status can never fully fill. The cunning mind might dismiss such matters as sentimental, but the wise strategist recognizes that personal authenticity bolsters professional credibility, and a balanced life fosters resilience in times of crisis.

So how does one actively cultivate a strategist's legacy? It begins with vision. Just as a criminal mind sees vulnerabilities others miss, and the legal mind foresees pitfalls others ignore, the legacy-driven strategist envisions outcomes that ripple decades into the future. They craft alliances that can self-sustain, secure policies that serve broader communities, and shape narratives that inspire not just immediate subordinates but the larger populace. Yet none of this is enough without the moral and ethical scaffolding that prevents your success from corroding under internal guilt or external scandal.

A legacy built without conscience is a structure of sand. When the wind of accountability arrives, it collapses into memory's dust."

Throughout our journey in this book, we have plumbed the depths of criminal psychology, studied the protective armor of law, and explored the hush of hidden maneuvers. In each chapter, a common thread has emerged: *balance*. The hustler's cunning, when reined by the attorney's precision, becomes unstoppable—yet remains susceptible to corruption if untempered by empathy and accountability. Now, on the cusp of concluding this exploration, we invite you to step beyond victory's fleeting glare and consider what kind of mark you will leave behind.

Perhaps you envision an expansive corporate empire, or you aim to revolutionize a social cause that has languished under bureaucracy. Maybe your ambition involves forging an entirely new field where your cunning and discipline combine into a breathtaking innovation. Whatever your goals, the final question is: *Will your influence stand as a beacon or a cautionary tale?* Will your name evoke admiration, trust, and the sense that you uplifted others? Or will it provoke memories of exploitation, cynicism, and empty grandeur undone by hubris?

That choice belongs to you alone, shaped by each deal you strike, each negotiation you orchestrate, each moral crossroad you confront. Criminal cunning and legal mastery can gift you extraordinary control, but they cannot define your heart. Only you can do that, through the daily practice of conscious reflection and the unwavering refusal to adopt methods that betray your deeper values.

At that award ceremony in the grand banquet hall, as applause crescendoed and the strategist accepted their glowing tribute, a moment arrived that will long be remembered. The honoree, gazing out at the crowd, quietly acknowledged the mentors who had taught them not only cunning but compassion, not only discipline but moral courage. In that instant, the applause became more than a mere accolade; it resonated with the sense that this person's legacy was not shaped by trickery or brute force alone, but by an equilibrium between ambition and integrity.

The cunning strategy is only half the story. The legacy it etches into hearts and societies is the other. Master both, and you wield a power that outlives your fleeting presence."

Such is the final call to action: let your strategist's spark burn brightly, guided by a deeper awareness of where each choice leads. If you fail, fail nobly, having upheld dignity rather than resorting to betrayal. If you succeed, allow your triumph to elevate others rather than crushing them. For in the twilight of your endeavors, when time slips away, the narrative that endures is the sum of actions taken when no one was looking, and the relationships nurtured or corroded by your approach to power.

And therein lies the heart of a strategist's legacy: *a bold blueprint for shaping the world on your own terms, bound by the awareness that everything you do echoes beyond your immediate gain.* Think like a criminal—fearless, inventive, untamed. Act like a lawyer—anchored, thoughtful, protected by legal armor. Yet above all, stand as a human being who cherishes the balance that allows power to be a force for enduring impact, rather than a dagger aimed at the collective good.

Carry your cunning with grace, shield it with law, and temper it with empathy. Only then can your legacy stand unbroken beneath the weight of its own ambition."

Conclusion

From Shadows to Spotlight

> The criminal mindset isn't about breaking laws—it's about breaking barriers to your success."

A hush falls upon the stage as the final speaker steps into a single spotlight. The audience—an eclectic mix of business magnates, legal experts, daring entrepreneurs, and everyday dreamers—waits in tense anticipation. Their eyes reflect a shared hunger for deeper understanding, for some ultimate truth that transcends stale self-help rhetoric and corporate jargon. Throughout the course of this journey, they have been riveted by tales of cunning thieves and razor-sharp attorneys, enthralled by the prospect that true power arises when predatory instincts merge with careful legal discipline. And now, at the turning of this final page, *Criminal Mindset: Think Like a Criminal and Act Like a Lawyer* must offer its concluding testament.

You, the reader who has traveled through these chapters, stand poised at a threshold. You have glimpsed how **Part I** unveiled the very foundations of a *criminal mindset*—the evolutionary impetus to outthink and outmaneuver, the cultivation of stealth, the relentless pursuit of opportunity even when it hides in plain sight. You absorbed how criminals exploit vulnerabilities, how they calibrate each move with predator-like acuity, and how they employ observation as the ultimate weapon. But those cunning instincts, unbridled by ethics or law, can twist into self-sabotage if left unchecked. Hence, you marched on into **Part II**, learning how the exacting armor of legal knowledge frames the cunning mind with essential boundaries. You witnessed that understanding the law is more than reciting statutes—it is an art of structuring your moves to stay protected, to negotiate with fierce clarity, and to navigate technicalities without drowning in them.

Then you crossed into **Part III**, *The Hustler's Playbook*, and realized that raw, strategic thinking flourishes even further when it spins through the code of alliances, invisible moves, and a studied quiet. You learned how to cloak your ambitions until the perfect moment, gleaning an advantage criminals exploit daily but that honest individuals often overlook. You saw how a hustler must know the rules of engagement, the art of forging alliances, and the virtues of staying under the radar to survive and thrive in an environment that can turn on them at any instant.

Lastly, **Part IV** brought you into the ethical crucible—the place where cunning and law confront the ghosts of conscience. You explored how power can blossom or corrupt, how each move to bend rules or exploit moral gray areas can morph into a slippery slope. You discovered that longevity in any game, be it the boardroom or the street, depends on preserving the balance between ambition and accountability. "*Walk the fine line,*" the chapters admonished, reminding you that the line dividing strategic brilliance from moral implosion can be perilously thin.

Now, at the culmination of it all, take a moment to weigh the lessons gleaned from criminals—*observational prowess, fearless innovation, and a willingness to question every assumed rule*—against the lawyer's creed—*respect for structure, an acute sense of boundaries, and the discipline to operate firmly within the safe corridors of law*. Let these two polarities unite within you, forging a dual approach that is as incisive as it is secure. In a world that grows ever more competitive, where cunning abounds yet so does scrutiny, this fusion endows you with a *rare vantage*: you can outmaneuver the naive and outlast the reckless.

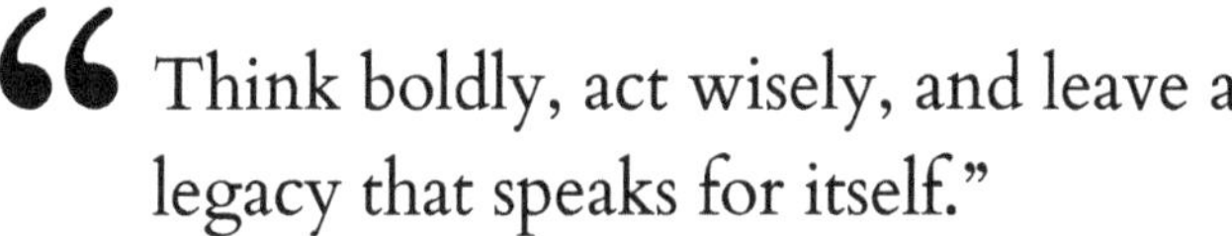

Why does legacy matter? Because *Criminal Mindset* is not a mere exercise in personal enrichment. It serves as a clarion call to harness your innate predatory instincts—to see the angles, to exploit the cracks, to seize hidden opportunities—*while* you uphold a commitment to a broader moral code. Criminals may enjoy short-lived success by ducking legal constraints, but their triumphs often unravel under the crushing weight of either law enforcement or betrayal from within. Lawyers might remain safely within the realm of statute and precedent, yet risk dulling their edge if they never dare to innovate or push beyond comfort.

The sweet spot emerges when you adopt the strengths of both realms—*the unflinching creativity of the criminal and the protective discipline of the lawyer.* That synergy makes you formidable. More importantly, if guided by an ethical anchor, it allows you to shape your world in ways that are not only prosperous but ultimately constructive. In the kaleidoscope of real life, where illusions abound and rules can be fluid, you become the strategist who does not flinch at adversity, but neither do you cast away principles for the sake of a quick advantage.

And what of fear—the fear of that ultimate downfall, the fear of losing control once you taste power? Indeed, power's seductive promise has toppled many who saw themselves as invincible. The difference lies in your decision to remain vigilant. If you have read these pages with sincerity, you now recognize the line between cunning and corruption is not a fixed one in the outside world; it resides in your conscience. Each day, you must decide whether the tactic you deploy—be it a stealthy negotiation, a cunning misdirection, or a calculated alliance—respects or disregards the core values that sustain community and personal integrity.

By stepping away from illusions of absolute control, you acknowledge that your power is meaningful only if it resonates beyond your self-interest. You can be the strategist who secures unstoppable deals, but also fosters alliances that stand the test of time. You can be the lawyer who disassembles opposition with deft legal artistry, but also remains unwavering in honesty. You can be the hustler who dominates the under-the-radar game, but also extends respect and loyalty to those who reciprocate.

In short, you can be a shape-shifter who manipulates circumstances, yet does not let manipulation become a way of life.

As you set this book aside—hopefully brimming with fresh perspectives and a renewed sense of potency—ask yourself: *What will my legacy be?* Will you be the enigma who left behind shattered alliances and scandal-ridden chapters in history, or the architect of a grander narrative—someone who rose above mediocrity by wielding cunning ethically, forging a path that others admire and continue? The choice rests in every subtle decision you make hereafter, in every quiet conversation or major confrontation, in each ambition you dare to chase or fear to dismiss.

In the end, we return to the essence that launched our exploration: criminals exploit rules, and lawyers enforce them. But you, dear reader, who stand to unite these two perspectives, can transcend that dichotomy altogether. You have not come here to replicate criminals or recite laws; you have come to harness the primal energy of creative thinking and discipline it with legal intelligence. That union, when fused with an ethical spine, births a new breed of leader—a strategist who can shape fortunes and ideas, repelling the forces of stagnation or brutality.

Let that final note ring in your mind: **"The criminal mindset isn't about breaking laws—it's about breaking barriers to your success,"** so long as you understand which boundaries must remain unbroken. Think like a criminal. Act like a lawyer. But live like a human being who has discovered that the richest power is one that neither cheats nor cowers—one that stands unwavering in self-awareness, moral accountability, and unwavering brilliance.

Go forward, then. Interweave cunning with compassion, discipline with daring, secrecy with just enough transparency to anchor trust. Perhaps your influence will shine openly, or perhaps it will grow in the quiet sanctuaries of behind-the-scenes negotiation. In either case, your ascendancy can be unassailable if you remember the cautionary tales of the fallen and the triumphs of those who wisely balanced ambition with moral clarity. This is your legacy in the making—*one that speaks volumes long after your voice has faded into the hush of history.*

Glossary

> "In the labyrinth where cunning and law intersect, definitions serve as stepping stones—each one guiding you further into strategic mastery."

Alliance

A cooperative relationship between two or more parties who temporarily link their resources, knowledge, or influence to achieve a shared objective. In criminal circles, alliances often form around mutually beneficial hustles or territorial concerns. In legitimate endeavors, alliances hinge on transparent agreements and legal structures. Yet regardless of setting, *the trust factor* can make or break any alliance, underscoring that the strongest bonds are rooted in clear boundaries and reciprocal benefit rather than manipulation or coercion.

Calculated Risk

A conscious decision to venture beyond the realm of safety, guided by analytical foresight and *a willingness to confront the unknown*. Criminals excel at risk analysis by instinct, often escaping capture through daring moves that appear foolhardy but are, in truth, meticulously weighed. Meanwhile, lawyers incorporate formal risk assessments to shield against legal pitfalls. The strategic mind merges these approaches, using both gut feeling and rational caution to achieve advantage without succumbing to unwarranted peril.

Criminal Mindset

A prism of sharp instincts and survival-based cunning that compels one to spot vulnerabilities, seize unguarded opportunities, and approach every scenario with predatory acuity. While this can devolve into lawbreaking if left unchecked, *the essence* of the criminal mindset is neither purely malevolent nor mindlessly destructive. It is, rather, an intense focus on *self-preservation and exploitation of weaknesses*—traits that can be ethically channeled into innovation and bold competition when tempered by legal awareness and moral considerations.

Ethos, Pathos, Logos

A triumvirate of rhetorical tools that shape persuasion.

- **Ethos** hinges on establishing credibility. Criminals often fabricate credentials to exude trust, whereas lawyers earn esteem through verifiable expertise and professional conduct.
- **Pathos** targets emotional resonance. Whether triggering pity or fear, it can sway decisions faster than logic alone.
- **Logos** embodies rational argumentation: facts, data, precedents, and case studies. Mastery of these three elements allows a strategist to *persuade diverse audiences* effectively, from jury boxes to clandestine deal-making environments.

Gray Areas

Legally and morally ambiguous zones where rules appear malleable or insufficiently defined. Criminals flock here, believing loopholes and technicalities lessen their risk of direct prosecution, while lawyers operate in these same spaces to redefine how laws are interpreted. Gray areas are not inherently unethical—*they are spaces ripe for creative maneuvering*, but can quickly morph into exploitative territory if left unchecked by self-imposed principle.

Hustler's Mindset

An approach that prizes relentless adaptability and opportunism, whether in the realm of crime or entrepreneurship. Hustlers operate on the premise that *no obstacle is insurmountable*, so long as one is clever enough to manipulate existing rules. The hustler's mindset thrives on improvisation, cunning observation, and perpetual motion. Yet, without ethical moorings, it risks spiraling into deceit and betrayal—a fate that undermines long-term success.

Legal Armor

A metaphor for the structured knowledge and procedural safeguards that shield an individual or organization from legal threats. It involves grasping statutes, case law, contractual nuances, and bureaucratic processes. By donning legal armor, you create *a protective boundary* around otherwise risky maneuvers—effectively turning precarious exploits into defensible strategies. Lawyers specialize in fortifying these protective layers; criminals who learn to emulate them stand a better chance of evading the full brunt of law enforcement.

Micro-expressions

Brief, involuntary facial indicators that betray one's underlying emotions before conscious masking can set in. Con artists and savvy negotiators alike rely on spotting micro-expressions to detect fear, eagerness, or uncertainty in their targets—allowing them to tailor responses and angles of persuasion with uncanny precision. Though fleeting, *these ripples of truth* can decisively shape the outcome of a heist, a courtroom cross-examination, or a high-stakes business negotiation.

Plausible Deniability

A state in which an individual can convincingly claim they lacked direct knowledge or involvement in a questionable action. Criminal masterminds often structure operations so that underlings handle incriminating tasks, insulating the top ranks from direct blame. Similarly, corporate leaders use layered bureaucracies and delegated sign-offs to evade accountability when ethical lines are breached. *Though a powerful protective tactic, plausible deniability can backfire* if overwhelming evidence or testimony exposes deliberate ignorance.

Power Dynamics

The shifting interplay of influence, authority, and control among individuals or groups. In underworld dealings, power dynamics manifest as territory disputes or leadership tussles resolved through intimidation or cunning. Lawyers observe similar struggles in legal proceedings, where each side contends for interpretive dominance. Recognizing who holds leverage, how alliances shift, and when to advance or retreat is *the essence of strategic mastery*, enabling you to maintain the upper hand even in volatile arenas.

Predator's Eye

The heightened awareness criminals use to size up *potential gains or threats* before making a move. This includes scrutinizing body language, scanning an environment's security weak points, and detecting the intangible pulse of fear or eagerness in a group. Lawyers mirror this skill in courtrooms, sensing jury reactions and calibrating arguments accordingly. A predator's eye is less about aggression and more about precise calculation: the knowledge that success hinges on *being one move ahead.*

Strategic Camouflage

A method of downplaying ambition, masking significant intentions behind ordinary appearances, or using diversionary tactics to operate unseen. Criminal enterprises leverage this by integrating into mundane societal roles—delivery personnel, low-profile tenants, unremarkable vehicles. Lawful professionals apply it through understated branding, discrete communications, or silent partnerships that enable them to develop projects away from prying eyes. *Success often hinges on blending in until the moment is ripe for a decisive reveal.*

Walking the Fine Line

An evocative phrase describing the precarious boundary between ethical ambition and moral compromise. Individuals who traverse this line harness cunning without succumbing to corruption, employing legal knowledge without strangling their sense of justice. Each subtle decision—whether to exploit a gray area, leverage a risky loophole, or push an alliance for personal gain—tests one's fortitude. *Walking the fine line* underscores the entire ethos of this book: achieving extraordinary power without sacrificing your conscience, reputation, or dignity along the way.

> Words are the skeleton of law and cunning, but definitions give them flesh and breath—use them well, for in their mastery lies your strongest shield."

In binding these terms and concepts together, this glossary serves as *the final puzzle piece* in your arsenal. Familiarize yourself with each definition, see how it weaves into the chapters you have read, and recall that the synergy of criminal insight and legal savvy—when anchored by morality—opens doors to a domain where *fear recedes, power grows*, and genuine legacy flourishes. With these words etched into your mind, may you move forward with heightened clarity, prepared to shape your future rather than be shaped by the illusions of a world that often mistakes cunning for cruelty and law for limitation.

Epilogue

> "Some legacies touch our lives not by direct embrace, but through the whispered tales that keep their spirit aflame."

As this journey of *Criminal Mindset* draws to a close, I find myself reflecting once more on the threads of family and memory that run through every page. Throughout these chapters, I have tried to fuse daring with discipline, cunning with conscience, always mindful of the inspirations that formed me. From my grandfather's steadfast resolve to my Chacha Ji's unwavering faith, I've derived the fuel to push boundaries while remaining anchored to a moral core. Yet there is another figure—one I know only through half-told stories, fleeting glimpses, and the reverent voices of those who cherish his memory: *my father, Sh. Mohan Veer Yadav.*

What little I know of him trickles through anecdotes passed down in hushed, awed tones—tales of a man whose aspirations gleamed beyond the horizon, who faced life's trials with a quiet determination. Some stories present him as a resolute soul who dreamed big but also carried the weight of family and duty upon his shoulders. Others describe flashes of stern leadership and stubbornness, painting a portrait of someone who wanted the best for me even before I could comprehend the meaning of ambition. In truth, I know him intimately and not at all, connected to him by a tapestry of stories rather than direct experience.

And yet I feel his presence in the spaces between what is said and what is left unsaid. There is an unmistakable sense that everything I accomplish carries his name forward in some invisible script. Perhaps his unspoken hopes echo in the challenges I choose to undertake, in the ambitions I dare to pursue, or in the moral lines I refuse to cross. Often, I wonder: *What aspirations might he have harbored for me?* Did he ever envision me walking the corridors of power or unraveling complexities beyond the average mind's grasp? Maybe he simply wanted me to be happy, stable, and principled. Whatever the precise dream, his legacy pulses in each choice I make, urging me toward a destiny that extends beyond my own reflection.

In the pages of this book, I have sought to share a mindset that marries the raw ingenuity of a risk-taker with the protective discipline of law. It stands to reason that in the quiet corners of that philosophy resides the essence of my father: a man whose spirit, I'm sure, would guide me to harness boldness and anchor it with empathy. If there is one silent prayer woven into these final paragraphs, it is that my life—and the paths I continue to forge—will honor him as much as they do my grandfather and Chacha Ji. To all three of them, I owe far more than I can ever repay; they are the unseen architects behind my courage, creativity, and conscience.

So I step forward, carrying his name like a promise. *Sh. Mohan Veer Yadav*: the stories I've heard, the aspirations left unvoiced—may they flow through me as I continue to evolve, learn, and create in this world. May I never lose sight of the foundation he helped lay, even if only through echoes. And may my journey—this book and everything that follows—stand testament to the boundless potential of a legacy that refuses to fade, no matter the distance or time.

Yours truly,

Vaibhav